MW00880425

YOU CAN UNDERSTAND THE REVELATION

Gene Keith

Third Printing – March 8, 2014

FORWARD

There is a great interest in prophecy today. Two of the most popular books are Daniel and The Revelation.

Did God really intend for laymen to understand this "strange" book?

Does The Revelation have any message for today or for the future?

Some people believe that The Revelation is simply a book of images and symbols, written mainly to encourage the suffering saints of the first century.

Others believe that Jesus returned to earth in AD 70, that Satan is bound, we are now living in the Kingdom, and the Revelation has no message for this generation.

Still others believe that the Second Coming of Jesus is still future, and that Jesus will literally return to this earth and reign on this earth for one thousand years.

For the first fourteen years of my ministry I was a "died in the wool" A-millennialist. I totally rejected the idea that Jesus would return to earth and reign on this earth for a literal one thousand years. In fact, the first term paper I wrote in college was titled, "Why there will be no Millennium."

I now believe that The Revelation *contains a message for the past, the present, and the future.*

We understand that many readers will not agree with our interpretation of this important book, but in all fairness, we will do our best to honestly and fairly provide our readers with the four most popular interpretations of this important book. We will present:

> The Roman Catholic interpretation
>
> The Reformers interpretation
>
> The Liberal interpretation, and
>
> The Conservative interpretation.

We are praying that God will richly bless you as you begin a study of one of the most interesting and most controversial books in the Bible.

Gene Keith

gk122532@gmail.com

CONTENTS

FIVE STATEMENTS ABOUT THE REVELATION

1. Don't call this book "Revelations" It is The Revelation.

2. Don't call it The "Revelation of John." It is The Revelation of Jesus Christ.

3. God wants us to understand this book (Revelation 1:1) *"The Revelation of Jesus Christ, which God gave unto him, to show unto his servants things which must shortly come to pass; and he sent and signified it by his angel unto his servant John."*

The Greek word, *Kalupto* means to cover or to hide. The Greek word *Apo* means to take away. Therefore, *the word Apokalupsis means* to take away the covering.

4. God intended for this book to be read, heard, and followed (Rev. 1:3). *"Blessed is he that readeth, and they that hear the words of this prophecy, and keep those things which are written therein: for the time is at hand."*

5. God explains *the purpose* of this book in (Rev. 1:19): *"Write the things which thou hast seen, and the things which are, and the things which shall be hereafter;*

Past

**"The *things which thou hast seen*, were things that were already in the past. John had seen them. They were history.

13

Present (John's day)

The things *which are,* were things that were *going on in John's day.*

Future

The things ***which would take place hereafter*** were things that are going to happen in the future.

THE REVELATION MAY ANSWER MANY POPULAR QUESTIONS

1. Did God really intend for laymen to understand The Revelation?

2. Why do some pastors believe in a Rapture and others do not?

3. Can Christ return before the whole world has heard the Gospel?

4. Will the church go through the Tribulation, or will there even be a literal Tribulation?

5. If Christ does come for His people, in what some believe is the *Rapture*, can anyone who has heard the Gospel and rejected it be saved after that?

6. Is the Roman Catholic Church the great harlot in The Revelation?

7. Is Mystery Babylon Rome, literal Babylon, or perhaps Mecca?

WHO WROTE THE REVELATION?

Who really wrote The Revelation? You will be surprised to learn how many modern commentaries will try to convince you that The Revelation was not written by the Apostle John, but by someone else. One Liberal Catholic woman teaches that John the Baptist wrote The Revelation and Christians later added the first three chapters. We don't take her seriously. Those who question the authorship of John usually do so along this line:

1. John's Name
The Apostle *John never calls himself* by his name in the Gospel of John. He uses expressions *as the disciple (John 21:24),* etc. In The Revelation, he refers to himself four times as "I. . . . John" (Rev. 1:9, 21:2, & 22:8).

2. The Grammar
The grammar is *different* in the Gospel of John and in The Revelation. One writer says "it is as different as Shakespeare and Huckleberry Finn."

Six Reasons We Believe John Wrote The Revelation

1) The *opening verses* of the book plainly claim that John was the author.

2) The early church Fathers believed John wrote the Revelation.[1]

3) No one questioned the authorship of John until Dionysius of Alexandria in the third century.

4) The reason Dionysius and others from Alexandria rejected John's authorship was Theological. The Alexandrian school followed Origen, the Father of the allegorical method of interpretation. Those men detested the idea of a literal 1000 year earthly Kingdom.

5) What about the grammar? The Gospel of John and The Revelation were written under entirely different circumstances. The Revelation was written in haste. John was told to write those things as he was seeing them. He didn't have time to "fine tune" the letter.

In addition to that, one writer mentions that John was thinking in Aramaic and writing in Greek.

6) In conclusion, we believe the evidence supports the fact that John wrote The Revelation. The burden of proof is on those who reject it.

---

[1]For a list of early church leaders, see John Walvoord, *The Revelation of Jesus Christ*, (Chicago: Moody Press, 1966) p. 12.

THE DATE OF THE REVELATION

There are two possible dates for the writing of The Revelation, and the date of the writing is a very important point. Conservative scholars favor a late date (90-100 A.D.), during the reign of the Roman Emperor Domition; Liberals favor an early date (62-70 A.D.) during the reign of Nero.

What difference does it make? Both of those Emperors persecuted the church. Liberals like the idea of an earlier date because it supports the Preterist interpretation of The Revelation.

Liberals and Preterists base their position on one lone statement attributed to one man, Papias, who said that the Apostle John was martyred before the destruction of Jerusalem in 70 AD.

The evidence however, is that John wrote it and he wrote it during the reign of Domition (95-100 AD). Several early church leaders lend support to this view..[2]

Clement of Alexandria wrote that John was in exile in Patmos but returned from the island.

Eusebius affirmed that John did return from exile following the death of Domition in A.D. 96.

---

[2] Walvoord, p. 13.

Irenaeus added to this the fact that John not only returned from exile on Patmos, but lived Ephesus during the reign of Trajan.

Again we ask, "What difference does it make when the book was written?" It makes a lot of difference. Liberal scholars like an early date to support the idea that much of The Revelation was fulfilled in the destruction of Jerusalem in A.D. 70 and has no future fulfillment. Liberals also favor the Preterist (past) approach to The Revelation.

FOUR WAYS TO INTERPRET THE REVELATION

1. The Roman Catholic interpretation (Preterist)

The Roman Catholic view is technically called the *Preterist* view. Preterism was introduced into the church by a Jesuit priest named Luis de Alcazar, who came up with this system of interpretation in order to defend the Catholic Church against attacks of the Reformers.. The word "praeter" means past. Therefore, those holding the Preterist view believe that Daniel and the Revelation were fulfilled in the past.

According to Preterists, all Bible prophecy has been fulfilled.

According to Preterism, events like the rise of the Antichrist, the tribulation, the Second Coming of Christ, and the Day of the Lord, all took place around 70 AD, the year the Romans invaded Jerusalem and destroyed the second Temple. The Second Coming was the *fall of Jerusalem* in AD 70.[3] There are actually four different groups of Preterists.

---

[3] Peter Ruckman, <u>The Book of Revelation</u>, (Pensacola: Pensacola Bible Press, 1970) p vii

The Neroian Preterists

Neroian Preterists believe that the things found in the Revelation were fulfilled in the days of the Roman Emperor, Nero (54-68 AD).

The Domitian Preterists

Domitian Preterists believe that the things written in the Revelation were fulfilled in the days of the Roman Emperor, Domition (81-96 AD).

Partial Preterists

Partial Preterists believe in a Second Coming and the resurrection of believers and the Judgment Seat of Christ. But Partial Preterists *do not believe* in the rapture, a literal Millennium, the Battle of Armageddon, a literal Anti-Christ, or a role for national Israel. Prominent partial Preterists include Gary DeMar, R.C. Sproul, Ken Gentry, and "The Bible Answerman," Hank Hanegraaff

Full (radical) Preterists

This group insists that all Bible prophecy has been fulfilled; nothing remains on the prophetic calendar. This radical preterism was championed by James Stuart Russell (1816-95), a Congregational clergyman in England. Russell authored a book titled, The Parousia, (from a Greek word meaning "coming" or "presence"), which first appeared in 1878.

Russell set forth the idea that the Second Coming of Christ, the judgment day, etc., are not future events at the end of the current dispensation. Rather, prophecies relating to these matters were fulfilled with Jerusalem's fall in A.D. 70. There is, therefore, no future "second coming" of Christ. Moreover, there will be no resurrection of the human body. Also, the final judgment and the end of the world have occurred already, with the destruction of Jerusalem.

Confuse Israel and the church: Preterists take the dangerous step of spiritualizing all passages of Scripture that relate to the nation of Israel, and claim that these refer to the church, the "New Israel."

2. The interpretation of the Reformers

This view is held by many important scholars such as: Wycliff, Luther, Bullinger, Brightman, Fox, Elliot, Barnes, Lord, Guinness, Carroll, and Sir Isaac Newton. Those who hold to this view believe The Revelation is a panorama of church and world history from the time of the Apostles until the consummation of the age.[4]

Those who hold this view try to make The Revelation "fit history," and they all interpret the Great Whore as the Roman Catholic Church and the Popes.

In the opinion of this present writer, *the Reformers were obsessed with that idea.* Here is an example of how they would interpret The Revelation.

- The First Beast was the Papacy. The Second Beast was the ecclesiastical power that sustained the Papacy.

- The Seven Vials were the seven "blows" at the power of the Papacy, such as the French Revolution,

---

[4] Criswell, p 25

23

the seizure of Rome by the French, and the capture of the Pope.

- The Great harlot is the Papacy.

- The Destruction of Babylon is the fall of the papacy.[5]

In the opinion of this present writer, there is one very great weakness in this approach, even though many notable scholars have embraced this view. There are at least fifty (50) different interpretations among those who hold this view and they all try to make the book "fit" their own time and place in history. For example: The **Falling Star in Revelation 9:1** has been interpreted to be an evil spirit, a Christian heretic, The Emperor Valens, Mohammed, and Napoleon.[6]

3. The Liberal interpretation

This is a method of interpreting the Bible *symbolically* rather than literally. This method was introduced into the church by a man named Origen from Alexandria who fiercely opposed the literal interpretation of the prophecies of the Kingdom.[7]

It is important to remember that the early church interpreted The Revelation *literally* for the first 250 years of church history and believed in a *literal reign* of Jesus Christ on the earth. It was the influence of Origen and St. Augustine, the Roman Catholic Theologian, who caused the orthodox approach to The Revelation to be lost for one

---

[5] Ray Summers, <u>Worthy is the Lamb</u>, (Nashville: Broadman, 1951) p 37

[6] Ruckman, p vii-viii

[7] J. Dwight Pentecost, *Outline of things to Come*, Grand Rapids: 1958, Zondervan, page 378.

thousand years.

Liberals look at The Revelation as merely *a message of hope* and encouragement for suffering Christians of the first century. Liberals do not see The Revelation as being actual events of the past r future, but rather symbols of the great struggle between good and evil.

It is important to stress again that from the time of Origen until the present, men who embrace the allegorical view do so *because they reject the doctrine of a literal reign of Jesus Christ on the earth as taught in Revelation 20:6.*

The "allegorical" position is not based on sound scholarship. It is the result of *rejecting the literal interpretation of God's Word.*

4. The Literal Interpretation

This brings us to the fourth view which we refer to as the correct interpretation. This position is called by some the "Futuristic" interpretation. As we stated several times already, this was the position of the early church for the first 250 years of church history. This approach takes the Bible literally and The Revelation literally.

Most of those who hold to this view believe in the Rapture, a literal tribulation, and a literal 1,000 year kingdom of peace on earth.

Those who hold this position take The Revelation literally unless there is a good reason to do otherwise. Rejecting the idea of a literal Kingdom is not a good reason to reject the literal interpretation of the Bible.

It is important to know that every major Evangelist and

Conservative Christian Writer since 1900 has held the Pre-millennial view:

Among them are men like: Evangelist Billy Sunday, Frank Norris, Hyman Appleman, Bob Jones Sr., M.R. DeHann, Lee Roberson, John R. Rice, Charles E. Fuller, Billy Graham, Dallas Billington, Jack Wertzon, Jack Van Impe, R. G. Lee, Adrian Rogers, Tim Lahaye, Dwight Pentecost, John Walvoord, and many others.

AN OUTLINE OF THE REVELATION

Here is a general outline of The Revelation held by those who take the Bible literally and are do not follow the teachings of Origen or St. Augustine, the Roman Catholic Theologian.

1. The Church Age (Revelation 1-3)

Everything we read in the first three chapters of The Revelation are related to the church. The churches mentioned in those chapters were seven real churches which existed in what is now called Turkey. The churches did not repent and now they are gone. Muslims control that part of the world now and it is a death sentence for a Muslim to convert to Christianity.

2. The "Rapture" of the Church (Revelation 4:1).

In our opinion, this verse marks the end of the church age. The word "church" does not appear again after this. There is a good reason for this. The church age is over. Consider the order of events here.

The verse begins with the words "After this." After what? After the church age which is described in chapters two and three. Where is the door opened? The door is opened in heaven. What did the voice say? The voice said, "Come up hither (here)!" What did the speaker say he was going to show John? The voice told John that he would see things that will take place hereafter."

3. The Tribulation Period (Revelation, chapters 4-19).

Everything in chapters 4-19 describe events which will transpire during the time called the Tribulation. Chapter 6 provides us with a complete outline of the Tribulation Period.

4. The Revelation (Revelation 19:11-21). This is where Jesus returns to earth accompanied by His saints.

There is a difference between the coming of Christ FOR His church and the coming of Christ WITH His church.

The **"Rapture"** is the coming of Christ **FOR** His people. This takes place in chapter four, verse one. **The "Revelation"** is the coming of Christ **WITH** His people. This takes place in chapter nineteen.

In the Rapture, when Jesus comes for His church, He comes like "a thief in the night." He could come at any time. His coming is imminent. **In the Revelation,** Jesus comes and "every eye shall see Him."

5. The Millennium (Revelation 20:1-6)

6. The Judgment Seat of Christ (Rev. 20:11-16)

7. The New Heaven and New Earth (Rev. 21-22)

CHAPTER 1

IN THE SPIRIT ON THE LORD'S DAY

"I, John, both your brother and companion in the tribulation and kingdom and patience of Jesus Christ, was on the island that is called Patmos for the word of God and for the testimony of Jesus Christ. 10 I was in the Spirit **on the Lord's Day** *"* (Rev. 1:9-10)

In the Spirit

John begins verse 10 by saying he was *in the spirit*. What did he mean by that? Walvoord says, "John's statement refers to his experience of being carried beyond normal sense into a state where God could reveal super-naturally the contents of the book." [8] John Walvoord mentions that Ezekiel (Ezek. 2:2, 3:12,14), Peter (10:10-11, 11:5), and Paul (Acts 22:17-18) had similar experiences.

On the Lord's Day

There are *two different opinions* on this verse. At first glance, we would assume John meant that this vision took place on Sunday. However, a closer look at the text might

---

[8] Ibid, p. 42

suggest otherwise.

What is this second opinion based on? Scholars remind us that even though Christians today regard Sunday as "the Lord's Day," nowhere in Scripture do we find Sunday called "The Lord's Day."

Walvoord reminds us that the day of Christ's resurrection is always referred to as "The first day of the week," and never as "the Lord's Day." (Matt. 28:1) (Mark 16:2) (Luke 24:1) (Acts 20:7) and (I Cor. 16:2). [9]

The best scholarship supports the idea that, rather than receiving his vision on Sunday, John was taken in the spirit to receive a revelation of the coming Day of The Lord."

The Day of the Lord

What exactly is *The Day of the Lord?* The Day of the Lord is that "extended period of time in which God will deal in judgment and sovereign rule over all the earth." [10] In our opinion, God pulled back the curtain of time and gave John a glimpse of coming events in prophecy.

We believe The Revelation includes the past, the present, and the future. We believe chapters 4-19 are still future.

---

[9] Walvoord, p. 42 .

[10] E.W. Bullinger, *The Apocalypse,* cited by John Walvoord, p 42.

CHAPTERS 2-3

THE MESSAGE TO THE SEVEN CHURCHES

We believe that these are seven real letters to seven real churches which once existed in what is now called Turkey. Although there are still a few Christians living there, the churches are gone and the land is under the control of Islam.

Read these letters carefully. Although these were real churches and they are gone now, the messages are as relevant as tomorrow morning's newspapers. Churches of every age have the same problems. Remember!

These letters are Christ's last message to His church. Jesus warns the churches of every age to *"Hear what the Spirit says to the churches."*

What is the Spirit warning the churches (and her members) to be concerned about?

1. Ephesus (Revelation 2:4): The danger of *losing our first love* for Christ.

2. Smyrna (Revelation 2:10): The danger of *fear of suffering* (Rev. 2:10).

3. Pergamos (Revelation 2:14-15): The danger of *doctrinal compromise.*

4. Thyatira (Revelation 2:20): The danger of *moral compromise.*

5. Sardis (Revelation 3:1-2): The danger of *spiritual deadness.*

6. Philadelphia (Revelation 3:11): The danger of *not holding fast.*

7. Laodecia (Revelation 3:15-16): The danger of *being lukewarm towards God.*

EPHESUS

THE CHURCH THAT LOST HER LOVE FOR GOD

We come now to the letters to the seven churches. Some have interpreted these letters as representing the seven ages of church history. This makes interesting preaching but, in the opinion of this present writer, does not represent the best scholarship.

Seven Real Churches

These were seven real letters to seven real churches which existed in Asia (Turkey) in the First Century. However, the problems addressed in these letters are present in churches of every age, so the warnings given here are always relevant.

It is also important to remember that these messages to the churches are the last words of Jesus Christ to His church. Christ's last message to the church in the Gospels is to *"Go ye therefore and teach all nations. . ."* (Matthew 28:19-20). His very last words to the church are *"Repent, or else!"*

Those interested in more historical details on the location of those seven churches and the situations in those cities may find Dr. Vernon McGee's commentaries helpful. You may also see pictures of the ruins of these cities on Google.

33

Revelation 2:1-5

"Write this letter to the angel of the church in Ephesus. This is the message from the one who holds the seven stars in his right hand, the one who walks among the seven gold lamp stands:

"I know all the things you do. I have seen your hard work and your patient endurance. I know you don't tolerate evil people.

You have examined the claims of those who say they are apostles but are not. You have discovered they are liars.

You have patiently suffered for me without quitting.

But I have this complaint against you. You don't love me or each other as you did at first! Look how far you have fallen from your first love!

Turn back to me again and work as you did at first.

If you don't, I will come and remove your lampstand from its place among the churches.

But there is this about you that is good: You hate the deeds of the immoral Nicolaitans, just as I do.

Anyone who is willing to hear should listen to the Spirit and understand what the Spirit is saying to the churches.

Everyone who is victorious will eat from the tree of life in the paradise of God."

The City

Ephesus was the most prominent city in the Roman province of Asia with a population of approximately 200,000 people. There was an outdoor theater there which could seat 20,000 people. Ephesus was also a resort city where the Roman Emperors came for vacations. The entire city was constructed of white marble. [11]

Paul's Ministry

The Apostle Paul ministered there for more than two years and experienced awesome results. Read (Acts 19:10) for the details. *"And this continued by the space of two years; so that all they which dwelt in Asia heard the word of the Lord Jesus, both Jews and Greeks."* There were about 25 million people in that area which were exposed to the Gospel through the ministry of Paul.

Temple of Diana

Ephesus was also the site of the great temple of Diana, which was one of the "Seven Wonders of the World." It was the largest Greek temple ever constructed. *Diana* was also worshiped by others who called her *Artemis.* Her cult is mentioned in the Bible, where some translations call it "Diana of the Ephesians" while others use "Artemis of the Ephesians." The idol's most extravagant temple was at Ephesus. It became one of the "seven wonders" of the ancient world. Constructed over the span of 220 years, of pure marble, it measured 345 feet x 105 meters long, by 165 feet x 50 meters wide, and was supported by massive columns each 55 feet x 17 meters high. Inside was a bizarre statue of the "fertility" idol, the original of which was apparently carved from a meteorite that had "fallen from heaven." (Acts 19:35)

Meteorites

It is not uncommon for meteorites to strike the earth. For example, in 1922, a 20-ton piece of space rock entered

---

[11]Vernon McGee <u>Thru the Bible, Vol V</u>, (Nashville: Thomas Nelson, 1983) p 899

earth's atmosphere and struck the ground near Blackston, Virginia (but no one made an idol out of it).

Paul's Influence

Paul's preaching has such an impact on idol worship that the silversmiths were worried that they would go out of business. Paul's influence on idol worship resulted in opposition from the silversmiths and a large riot (Acts 19:25-27).

23 And the same time there arose no small stir about that way.

24For a certain man named Demetrius, a silversmith, which made silver shrines for Diana, brought no small gain unto the craftsmen;

25Whom he called together with the workmen of like occupation, and said, Sirs, ye know that by this craft we have our wealth.

26Moreover ye see and hear, that not alone at Ephesus, but almost throughout all Asia, this Paul hath persuaded and turned away much people, saying that they be no gods, which are made with hands:

27So that not only this our craft is in danger to be set at nought; but also that the temple of the great goddess Diana should be despised, and her magnificence should be destroyed, whom all Asia and the world worshippeth.

28And when they heard these sayings, they were full of wrath, and cried out, saying, Great is Diana of the Ephesians.

29And the whole city was filled with confusion: and having caught Gaius and Aristarchus, men of Macedonia, Paul's companions in travel, they rushed with one accord into the theater.

³⁰And when Paul would have entered in unto the people, the disciples suffered him not.

³¹And certain of the chief of Asia, which were his friends, sent unto him, desiring him that he would not adventure himself into the theater.

³²Some therefore cried one thing, and some another: for the assembly was confused; and the more part knew not wherefore they were come together.

³³And they drew Alexander out of the multitude, the Jews putting him forward. And Alexander beckoned with the hand, and would have made his defense unto the people.

³⁴But when they knew that he was a Jew, all with one voice about the space of two hours cried out, great is Diana of the Ephesians.

³⁵And when the town clerk had appeased the people, he said, Ye men of Ephesus, what man is there that knoweth not how that the city of the Ephesians is a worshipper of the great goddess Diana, and of the image which fell down from Jupiter?

36 Seeing then that these things cannot be spoken against, ye ought to be quiet, and to do nothing rashly.

37 For ye have brought hither these men, which are neither robbers of churches, nor yet blasphemers of your goddess.

38 Wherefore if Demetrius, and the craftsmen which are with him, have a matter against any man, the law is open, and there are deputies: let them implead one another.

39 But if ye inquire anything concerning other matters, it shall be determined in a lawful assembly.

40 For we are in danger to be called in question for this day's

uproar, there being no cause whereby we may give an account of this concourse.

41 And when he had thus spoken, he dismissed the assembly."

Commendation

Notice all of the good things Christ commended this church for (2-4). *²I know thy works, and thy labor, and thy patience, and how thou canst not bear them which are evil: and thou hast tried them which say they are apostles, and are not, and hast found them liars: ³And hast borne, and hast patience, and for my name's sake hast labored, and hast not fainted."*

Nicolaitanes

Christ also commended them for hating the doctrine of the Nicolaitanes (2:6). *⁶But this thou hast, that thou hatest the deeds of the Nicolaitanes, which I also hate."*

TWO POPULAR INTERPRETATIONS

1. Popes and Bishops

The Greek word *Nikao* means "conquer." The word *Laos* means "the people." The word Nicolaitane means "conquering the people." Some believe the **Nicolaitanes** to be the forerunners of the clerical hierarchy (Priests and Popes) who began to "Lord it over" the laymen in the church.

2. Immoral Living

Another interpretation is that the Nicolaitanes were **licentious sect** in the church which encouraged church members to participate in the heathen feasts which involved free love (orgies).[12]

---

[12] John Walvoord, <u>The Revelation of Jesus Christ</u>, (Chicago: Moody

THE BIG PROBLEM IN EPHESUS

Their Love Had Grown Cold

4Nevertheless I have somewhat against thee, because thou hast left thy first love.

5Remember therefore from whence thou art fallen, and repent, and do the first works; or else I will come unto thee quickly, and will remove thy candlestick out of his place, except thou repent."

This is thirty years after Paul's fruitful ministry (Acts 19) and the church is filled with second-generation Christians. John Walvoord reminds down through history, the church experiences a similar (downward) trend.

- Love for God begins to cool off.

- Then our love for God is replaced by love of the things of the world.

- This is followed by compromise and spiritual corruption.

- This is followed by a departure from the faith.

THE IMPORTANCE OF LOVING GOD

(Matthew 22:35-40). 35Then one of them, which was a lawyer, asked him a question, tempting him, and saying,

36Master, which is the great commandment in the law?

37Jesus said unto him, Thou shalt love the Lord thy God with all thy heart, and with all thy soul, and with all of thy mind.

Press, 1966) p 58

[38]*This is the first and great commandment*

[39]*And the second is like unto it, Thou shalt love thy neighbor as thyself.* [40]On these two commandments hang all the law and the prophets."

FIVE THINGS WHICH WE MAY LOVE IN THE PLACE OF GOD

1. Love of Money (1 Tim. 6:10)

"For the love of money is the root of all evil: which while some coveted after, they have erred from the faith, and pierced themselves through with many sorrows."

2. Love of this World (1 John 2:15-16)

"Love not the world, neither the things that are in the world. If any man love the world, the love of the Father is not in him.

For all that is in the world, the lust of the flesh, and the lust of the eyes, and the pride of life, is not of the Father, but is of the world."

"Stop loving this evil world and all that it offers you, for when you love the world, you show that you do not have the love of the Father in you.

For the world offers only the lust for physical pleasure, the lust for everything we see, and pride in our possessions. These are not from the Father. They are from this evil world." (NLT)

3. Love of Material Things (1 John 5:21). *"Little children, keep yourselves from idols."*

4. Love of Parents and/or children (Matt. 10:37).

"But whosoever shall deny me before men, him will I also deny before my Father which is in heaven.

34Think not that I am come to send peace on earth: I came not to send peace, but a sword.

35For I am come to set a man at variance against his father, and the daughter against her mother, and the daughter in law against her mother in law.

36And a man's foes shall be they of his own household.

37He that loveth father or mother more than me is not worthy of me: and he that loveth son or daughter more than me is not worthy of me."

5. Love of Husbands and/or wives (First Corinthians 7:34).

"But he that is married careth for the things that are of the world, how he may please his wife.

34There is difference also between a wife and a virgin. The unmarried woman careth for the things of the Lord, that she may be holy both in body and in spirit: but she that is married careth for the things of the world, how she may please her husband.

35And this I speak for your own profit; not that I may cast a snare upon you, but for that which is comely, and that ye may attend upon the Lord without distraction."

CHRIST'S LAST WARNING TO THE CHURCH

(Revelation 2:4) *Nevertheless I have somewhat against thee, because thou hast left thy first love. Remember therefore from whence thou art fallen, and repent, and do the first works; or else I will come unto thee quickly, and will remove thy candlestick out of his place, except thou repent."*

The church in Ephesus retained its vigor for several centuries and was not only the seat of Eastern bishops but also the meeting place of the third General Council in A.D. 431. After that, the city declined and in fourteenth century, the Turks deported its remaining inhabitants. The ruins of the city are now located seven miles from the sea.

Those churches are gone now. All that is left of them is ruins. Tourists who wish to see them are directed by Muslim guides.

TV COMEDY "LITTLE MOSQUE ON THE PRAIRIE"
By Moody Adams (2007)

Why is a very mediocre Canadian-produced TV sitcom, attracting huge interest world-wide? "The answer, of course, lies in its provocative title," writes Alan Ferguson in The Province. "The launch last week of CBC's Little Mosque on the Prairie drew media crews from Britain, the U.S. and around the world." The storyline hinges on the attempts of a community of Muslims to establish themselves in the fictional Prairie town of Mercy, Sask. The

Muslims are nice friendly people.

The non-Muslim are portrayed as funny, bigoted, bumpkins who are suspicious of Muslims.

This politically correct production aims at gaining acceptance of Islam in the same way homosexuals did — by getting the audience to laugh at them.

CBC must have lost its mind if they think people will laugh at a religion that teaches women are inferior to men (Koran 4:34), that slaves are a gift from Allah (Koran 33:50), that Jews are inhuman apes (2:65), and that beheading "infidels" guarantees you will go to heaven (Koran 47:4-6).

In a final irony, the show premiered on the week the U.N. announced Muslim terrorists have killed 30,000 Iraqis in the past year. Have you started laughing yet?

SMYRNA

THE SUFFERING CHURCH

Revelation 2:8-11

8 "And to the angel of the church in Smyrna write, These things says the First and the Last, who was dead, and came to life:

9 I know your works, tribulation, and poverty (but you are rich); and I know the blasphemy of those who say they are Jews and are not, but are a synagogue of Satan.

10 Do not fear any of those things which you are about to suffer. Indeed, the devil is about to throw some of you into prison, that you may be tested, and you will have tribulation ten days. Be faithful until death, and I will give you the crown of life.

11 He who has an ear, let him hear what the Spirit says to the churches. He who overcomes shall not be hurt by the second death."

Seven Real Churches

In our opinion, chapters two and three of the Revelation are seven literal letters to seven real churches which exited in Asia (modern day Turkey) in the first century.

Common Problems

Those seven churches had problems which have been experienced by churches in every generation.

Last Message to His Church

It is also important to mention that these seven messages are the very last words of Jesus Christ to His church. Christ warned the churches to repent or He would remove their church. They didn't repent and He did remove their churches.

Conquered by Islam

That area of the world which was once the center of Christianity is now under the rule of Islam, the religion of the sword.

The church of our generation would do well to heed the warnings found in these two chapters.

The City is now Izmir, Turkey

Vernon McGee reminds us that the city of Smyrna is still in existence in our day. It is the Turkish city of Izmir. Smyrna was one of the most beautiful cities in Asia. There was a large beautiful harbor there and large theater and a music center. Smyrna was the "Home of Music." There was also a large stadium located in Smyrna. It was in that very stadium that Polycarp, a disciple of the Apostle John, was burned alive in A.D. 155.[13]

---

[13]Vernon McGee, p 904

46

Pastor Polycarp

Polycarp, the famous early church father was the pastor of the church in Smyrna for many years. He was finally burned at the stake in the very city where he had served as pastor. When the heathen judges gave him a chance to renounce his faith and life, here is what he said: *"Four score and six years have I served the Lord and He never wronged me: How then can I blaspheme my King and Savior?"*[14]

The example of this faithful pastor had a great influence on this church and it remained faithful to Christ for years. Smyrna and Philadelphia are the only two churches which have had a continuous existence since that day.

A Good Church

Smyrna and Philadelphia are the only two of these seven churches Christ does not find anything to condemn. This church was busy working for Christ.

A Poor/Rich Church

Vernon McGee reminds us that the Smyrna congregation was composed of ex-slaves, runaway slaves, freed slaves, poor people, *and those who had lost everything they had when they became Christians.* This congregation may have been poor by the world's standards, but in God's eyes, they were very rich.

A Persecuted Church

They were not only going through severe trials at that time, the Lord warns them in this letter that there were more trials to come and they were to be faithful, even unto

---

[14] John Walvoord, The Revelation of Jesus Christ, page 64

death.

Historians tell us that millions[15] of Christians died during those days of persecution of the early church.

Persecuted 10 Days

According to Vernon McGee, there were ten periods of persecution under ten different Roman Emperors.[16]

The Crown of Life

Jesus told them that those who were faithful would receive a "crown" of life. Salvation is a free gift, but rewards (crowns) were awarded for faithful service.

---

[15]Fox Book of Martyrs estimates that 5 million were martyred during this period.

[16] McGee, page 906.

FIVE CROWNS AVAILABLE TO BELIEVERS

There are at least five (5) crowns **available** to believers for their faithful service to our Lord. It is also important to mention at this point that although salvation cannot be lost, crowns can be lost or not earned. For a better understanding of these "crowns," read: 1 Cor. 9:25, 1 Thess. 2:19, 2 Tim. 4:8, James 1:12, 1 Peter 5:4, Rev. 2:10, Rev. 3:11, and Rev. 4:10.

The Second Death

Jesus told us not to fear those who could kill the body, but not our souls, but to fear Him (God) who could destroy both soul and body in hell (Matthew 10:28). Those faithful people who had died as martyrs would never have to worry about dying again. Their dying was over and their suffering was behind them. The second death is for the unsaved and believers should never worry about that.

D. L. Moody once said that *if we are born only once, we must die twice. If we are born twice, we only die once (physical death). In fact, if we are born twice we may not even die at all if Christ returns in our lifetime.*

The Only Warning

The only warning Jesus gave this church was *not to fear* the things they were about to suffer. Their sufferings would soon be over and they would never suffer again. This "Tribulation" they were about to suffer was not "The Great

Tribulation." The church will not be left on earth to endure that. We will discuss The Great Tribulation in detail at a later date.

PERGAMOS

THE CHURCH AT SATAN'S HEADQUARTERS

(Rev. 2:12-17) *"And to the angel of the church in Pergamos write, 'These things says He who has the sharp two-edged sword:*

13 I know your works, and where you dwell, where Satan's throne is. And you hold fast to My name, and did not deny My faith even in the days in which Antipas was My faithful martyr, who was killed among you, where Satan dwells.

14 But I have a few things against you, because you have there, those who hold the doctrine of Balaam, who taught Balak to put a stumbling block before the children of Israel, to eat things sacrificed to idols, and to commit sexual immorality.

15 Thus you also have those who hold the doctrine of the Nicolaitans, which thing I hate.

16 Repent, or else I will come to you quickly and will fight against them with the sword of My mouth.

17 He who has an ear, let him hear what the Spirit says to the churches. To him who overcomes I will give some of the hidden manna to eat. And I will give him a white stone, and on the stone a new name written which no one knows except him who receives it."

The City of Pergamos

Ephesus was the commercial center. Smyna, now named Izsmir, was the commercial center, and Pergamos was the religious center. Pergamos was the home of the greatest library in the pagan world with over 200,000 volumes. In fact, the name "Pergamos" came from the word "parchment" (pergamena) or paper, the use of which originated there.

Satan's Throne

Pergamos was the center of pagan worship. Jesus called it "Satan's headquarters." There were temples to several pagan gods in the city of Pergamos. There were alters and temples of: Athena, Zeus, Dionysius (also called Bachus). Bachus was pictured as the goat-god. The upper part of this idol looked like a man and the lower part looked like a goat with cloven feet and a tail. The picture of Satan with horns etc. did not come from the Bible. *It came from Pergamos and pagan Asia.*

A Famous Hospital

Pergamos was also home of the largest hospital in the ancient world. Some would call it the "Mayo Clinic" of Asia. This hospital was actually a temple to Asklepois. Vernon McGee describes this hospital this way:

The construction of the temple was unusual in that it was round. There they used every means of healing imaginable. They used medicine and psychology - - and about everything else.

Put yourself in this situation. You go down long tunnels, and above are holes that look like air holes for ventilation but they are not. As you walk along these tunnels, sexy voices come down through those holes, saying to you, 'you are going to get well. You are going to feel better. You are going to be healed.

Then, you go down to the hot baths where you get a massage. Then there was a little theater where they watched plays on healing.

If they hadn't healed you by then, they put the patient in the temple at night and turned loose nonpoisonous snakes that crawled over them (that was their shock treatment back then).

They had a back door through which they carried out the dead.

Caesar Augustus used to go there. He was an alcoholic and they dried him out every year."

Problems at Pergamos

There were two things wrong with the church at Pergamum. The doctrine of Balaam and the doctrine of the Nicolaitans.

1. Doctrine of Balaam" Vernon McGee makes a difference between:

- The **doctrine** of Balaam;
- The **error** of Balaam (Jude 11), and
- The **way** of Balaam (2 Peter 2:15).

The prophet Balaam loved money. He was guilty of covetousness. The enemies of Israel tried to hire this prophet to curse Israel. He first declined, but when they offered him more money, the money-loving prophet decided to "pray about it." There's more to the story.

Doctrine refers to teaching

The prophet Balaam taught the enemies of God to corrupt Israel by encouraging the Jewish men to "date" and to marry the Moabite women. The Moabites were very immoral people and when the young men of Israel began to date and marry them and the rest is history. **The doctrine of Balaam** is teaching people in the church to compromise morally, to marry heathen wives, to engage in sexual sins, and to produce heathen children.

The Nicolaitans

This is the second time this sin has come up. The church in Ephesus was commended for hating it like God did. The church in Permamos was "holding it" (practicing it) even though God hated it. There are two different interpretations of this.

1. Priests and Popes

The Greek word *Nikao* means "conquer." *laos* means "the people." The word Nicolaitane means "conquering the people." Some believe the Nicolaitanes to be the forerunners of the clerical hierarchy (Priests and Popes) who began to "Lord it over" the laymen in the church.

2. Immoral Living

Another interpretation is that the Nicolaitanes were a licentious sect in the church which encouraged church members to participate in the heathen feasts which involved free love and gross immorality (orgies).17 The attitude of some of the people in that congregation was: "If it feels good . . . do it!"

A Very Sad Story

Someone said: "The blood of the martyrs is the seed of the church." The church exploded during persecution. But with the "so called" conversion of Constantine, the church began to decline and never recovered. When Rome ceased to persecute the church it became popular to be a Christian. The church became friendly so friendly with the government it became difficult to maintain a distinction between the church and the world.

John Walvoord describes it this way: *"The history of the three centuries which followed is a record of increasing corruption of the church, departure from biblical doctrine, and a an attempt to combine Christian theology with pagan philosophy.*

As a result, the church soon lost its hope in the early return of Christ, and biblical simplicity was replaced by a complicated church organization which substituted human creeds and the worship of Mary, the mother of our Lord, for true Biblical doctrine. The church committed the same sin of which Israel was guilty in the Old Testament, namely the worship or idols, and union with the heathen world. The solemn warning to the church given to the church was forgotten." 18

---

[17] John Walvoord, <u>The Revelation of Jesus Christ</u>, (Chicago: Moody Press, 1966) p 58

THYATIRA

THE CHURCH WITH THE SEXY WOMAN TEACHER

(Rev. 2:18-29) *18 "And to the angel of the church in Thyatira write,' These things says the Son of God, who has eyes like a flame of fire, and His feet like fine brass:*

19 I know your works, love, service, faith, and your patience; and as for your works, the last are more than the first.

20 Nevertheless I have a few things against you, because you allow that woman Jezebel, who calls herself a prophetess, to teach and seduce my servants to commit sexual immorality and eat things sacrificed to idols.

21 And I gave her time to repent of her sexual immorality, and she did not repent.

22 Indeed I will cast her into a sickbed, and those who commit adultery with her into great tribulation, unless they repent of their deeds.

23 I will kill her children with death, and all the churches shall know that I am He who searches the minds and hearts. And I will give to each one of you according to your works.

24 Now to you I say, and to the rest in Thyatira, as many as do not have this doctrine, who have not known the depths of Satan, as they say, I will put on you no other burden.

25 But hold fast what you have till I come.

26 And he who overcomes, and keeps My works until the end, to him I will give power over the nations

27 'He shall rule them with a rod of iron; They shall be dashed to pieces like the potter's vessels'-- as I also have received from My Father;

28 and I will give him the morning star.

29 He who has an ear, let him hear what the Spirit says to the churches."

The City of Thyatira

Thyatira was the smallest of the seven churches, located in the smallest city and yet they received the longest letter. In fact, it was the most severe of the seven letters. The only other mention of the city of Thyatira is in Acts 16:14-15, where it is mentioned as the home of Lydia. The reference also mentions that Lydia was a seller of purple. Thyatira was famous for the manufacture of purple dye.

The Church at Thyatira

Evidently Lydia took the Gospel back to Thyatira after being converted after attending a Bible study in which Paul was present. We have no record of any other evangelistic efforts there.

Commendation

The church at Thyatira was a hard working church. They were commended for their love. This is the word "charity," for which none of the other churches were commended for. They performed faithful service to God. They exercised true faith. They had patience. This means they had worked hard and had not quit.

Jezebel

The church at Thyatira had a major problem. They were allowing a person Jesus called "Jezebel," to hold a position of leadership in the church and she had led the congregation into extremely sinful conduct. The original Jezebel was perhaps the most evil woman in the Old Testament. She was the heathen wife of King Ahab of Israel.

- Jezebel attempted to combine the worship of the idol Baal with the worship of Jehovah.

- Jezebel tried to stamp out the worship of Jehovah (1 Kings 16:33).

- Jezebel tried to kill all of the true prophets of God including Elijah (19:2).

- Jezebel was finally killed and her was body eaten by dogs (2 Kings 9:33-35).

- Jezebel was so evil the dogs wouldn't eat her hands or her head.

There is reason to believe that the Jezebel mentioned in this letter was not an ordinary church member, but possibly the pastor's wife.18 This Jezebel claimed to be a prophetess and held a position of leadership in that church.

---

[18] See Walvoords' reason for this position. Page 73.

This Jezebel was also a very immoral woman and many of the members of that congregation were following her and living immoral lives.

Adultery

Fornication is mentioned several times in The Revelation, but this is the only place where "adultery" is mentioned. This is a specific reference to breaking marriage vows. *"Marriage is honorable in all, and the bed undefiled: but whoremongers and adulterers God will judge"* (Heb. 13:4). It is difficult for modern readers to fully understand the depth of immorality in that city without understanding the immorality of the pagan religions of that time. Nearly all false religions find some way to combine religion with sexual immorality. Thus pagan worship often included sex orgies as a part of the rituals.

A Warning to the Church

Since Jezebel liked the bedroom so much, God was going to judge her by confining her to another kind of bed: *a hospital bed (sickbed).* God would send tribulation upon them. God would kill her children (those who were following her immoral behavior and teaching). This present age has become obsessed with sex. It would be good for those in the church today to remember God's warnings to those who are engaging in lust, fornication and adultery.

TWO VERY DANGEROUS SINS IN THE CHURCH

- The large number of women in church history who have seduced the church into following false doctrines.

- Sexual immorality in the church today.

- This may be offensive to some readers but the truth is the truth.

1. False preachers prey on women (2 Timothy 3:5-8)

5 *"They will act as if they are religious, but they will reject the power that could make them godly. You must stay away from people like that.*

6 *They are the kind who work their way into people's homes and win the confidence of vulnerable women who are burdened with the guilt of sin and controlled by many desires.*

7 *Such women are forever following new teachings, but they never understand the truth. 8 And these teachers fight the truth just as Jannes and Jambres fought against Moses. Their minds are depraved, and their faith is counterfeit. "*

2. People (not just women) who are living in sin are more vulnerable to false doctrine.

Read 6-7 again. 6 They are the kind who work their way into people's homes and **win the confidence** of vulnerable women who are burdened with the guilt of sin and controlled by many desires. 7 **Such women** are forever following new teachings, but they never understand the truth.

THOUGHTS ABOUT WOMEN PREACHERS
By the late Dr. John R. Rice

"So it is with women preachers. They do good, but how much harm they do! First, the rise of women preachers has meant the rise of multiplies sects of people with false doctrines of every kind. The Fox sisters and Spiritism, Mrs. White and Seventh Day Adventism, Mrs. Mary Baker Eddy and Christian Science, Mrs. Filmore and Unity, Mrs. Aimee Semple McPherson and the so-called 'Foursquare

Gospel,' Pentecostalism and its vast majority of women preachers with the blight of sinless perfection doctrine, radical emotionalism, 'speaking in tongues' and trances, its overemphasis on healing that leads thousands to despair after false pretenses of healing — these things surely should warn us that there is infinite harm in women preaching."

(Source: Bobbed Hair, Bossy Wives and Women Preachers; by Dr. John R. Rice; pg. 58; Sword of the Lord Publishers, P.O. Box 1099, Murfreesboro, TN, 37133; copyright 1941; ISBN: 0-87398-065-4)

FAMOUS WOMEN PREACHERS

1. Agnes Osman = Speaking in Tongues

Nobody in the United States of America had ever spoken in tongues 1901. The practice of speaking in tongues was introduced into in the United States in 1901, by a woman at Bethel College, Topeka, Kansas.

This woman, Agnes Ozman, claimed to have received what she called the "baptism of the Spirit" and spoke in tongues. Following her experience, the practice of speaking in tongues soon became a part of the Holiness movement in the United States.

2. Evangelist Aimee Semple McPherson

"Aimee Semple McPherson in the 1920s, allegedly faked her own death. She later claimed that she had been kidnapped, but a grand jury could neither prove that a kidnapping occurred, nor that she had faked it. Roberta Semple Salter, her daughter from her first marriage, became estranged from Semple

McPherson and successfully sued her mother's attorney for slander during the 1930s. As a result of this she was cut out of her mother's will. *Aimee Semple McPherson died in 1944 from an accidental overdose of* barbiturates.*"* (Google)

3. Prophetess Mary Baker Eddy

Mary Baker Eddy is the founder of the cult known as "Christian Science," which is neither Christian or Science. Mrs. Eddy was chronically sick growing up, with many ailments including paralysis, hysteria, seizures and convulsions.

At 22, she married her first of three husbands, George Glover, who died within 6 months from yellow fever.

Following Glover's death, she began to be involved in mesmerism (hypnosis) and the occult practices of spiritualism and clairvoyance (Ruth Tucker, Another Gospel, p. 152).

Still ill, she married Daniel Patterson in 1853, a dentist and homeopathic practitioner. It was at this time she met mental healer Phineas P. Quimby (1802-1866), whose influence would shape her belief of Christian Science.

Quimby believed that illness and disease could be cured through positive thoughts and healthy attitudes, *by changing one's beliefs about the illness.*

3. "Pastor" Florence Louise Crawford (Church of God – Tennessee).

Florence Crawford (1872-1936) was the founder and general overseer of the APOSTOLIC FAITH CHURCH. She had a spiritual experience in 1906 at the Azusa Street Mission and began preaching soon thereafter.

She left her husband of sixteen years and made a series of evangelistic trips to the Northwest and Canada.

In 1908 Crawford and her friend, Clara Lum, stole the 50,000-person mailing list for William Seymour's paper, Apostolic Faith, and moved to Portland, Oregon. This crippled Seymour's ministry. The reason given for this strange act was that they did not agree with Seymour's marriage to Jenny Moore because they were convinced time was too short before the Rapture.

The congregation which eventually grew into the Pentecostal denominations the CHURCH OF GOD (Cleveland, Tennessee) and the CHURCH OF GOD OF PROPHECY, was formed in 1906.

4. "Pastor" Pheobe Palmer = Sinless Perfectionism.

"Women were leaders in the holiness or sinless perfection movement of the last half of the 19th century.

This was the movement out of which the Pentecostal movement grew. One of the leading proponents of holiness doctrine in Methodism was Mrs. Phoebe Palmer and her husband, Dr. Walter Palmer." (Vinson Synan, The Holiness-Pentecostal Tradition, p. 17).

5. Mrs. Sarah Lankford = Complete Sanctification

"It was another woman, Mrs. Sarah A Lankford, who won the Palmers over to the idea of complete sanctification in 1839. Mrs. Lankford held meetings in her home, and Mrs. Palmer became the leader of the meetings after her "sanctification."

Mrs. Palmer taught that when the Christian put all on the altar, "one could be instantly sanctified through the

64

baptism of the Holy Ghost."

This refers to a type of sinless perfectionism that was erroneously promoted. Phoebe Palmer had a vast influence through her speaking ministry and writings.

6. Prophetess Ellen G. White = Seventh Day Adventists

Seventh Day Adventists depend heavily on the writings of Ellen White.

They believe those of us who worship on Sunday have the Mark of the Beast. Ellen White promoted vegetarianism.

For example, in 1938 the SDA Church compiled Ellen White's writings on health into a book entitled *Counsels on Diets and Foods.*

The following quotation is taken from that book: *"Butter and meat stimulate. These have injured the stomach and perverted the taste. The sensitive nerves of the brain have been benumbed, and the animal appetite strengthened at the expense of the moral and intellectual faculties* (p 48). (ww.nonsda.org/study11.shtml)

7. Kathryn Khulman = Fake Healer

Benny Hinn learned his "slain in the spirit" techniques from Kathryn Khulman. In a shocking revelation sure to rock millions in the Christian community Hinn, 57, recently sneaked off to a romantic Roman holiday in the Eternal City with another beautiful blonde evangelist! The multi-millionaire Bible-thumping faith healing TV host of *This Is Your Day* was caught walking hand in hand with his secret lover where he was checked into the presidential suit in a top hotel under an assumed name right out of the

Old Testament!

http://blogs.ocweekly.com/navelgazing/2010/07/benny
_hinn_paula_white_affair.php)

8. "Pastor" Marilyn Hickey

Pastor Marilyn Hickey (author of God's Seven Keys to Make You Rich) is another Pentecostal leader today. She pastors a church in Colorado, has written many popular books, and frequently preaches at large conferences. When false prophet, Rodney Howard-Browne conducted his "laughing revival" crusade at Carpenter's Home Church in Lakeland, Florida, in 1993, Hickey flew to the meetings and spent her time there on the floor laughing hysterically.

When Howard-Browne called this Pentecostal female preacher to the microphone, she laughed and fell down and could not speak (Charles and Frances Hunter, Holy Laughter, 1994, p. 35).

9. "Pastor" Joyce Meyer

"On November 11, 2003, the St. Louis Post Dispatch published a four part series exposing Meyer's $10 million corporate jet, her husband's $107,000 silver-gray Mercedes sedan, her then $2 million home and houses worth another $2 million for her four children, her $20 million headquarters, furnished with "$5.7 million worth of furniture, artwork, glassware, and the latest equipment and machinery, including a malachite round table, a marble-topped antique commode, a custom office bookcase, a $7,000 Stations of the Cross in Dresden porcelain, an eagle sculpture on a pedestal, another eagle made of silver, and numerous paintings. " (Google)

ARE WOMEN PASTORS BIBLICAL?

We believe that men and woman are spiritually equal in position before God but that God has ordained distinct and separate spiritual functions for men and women in the home and the church. The husband is to be the leader of the home and men are to be the leaders (pastors and deacons) of the church. Accordingly, only men are eligible to be licensed and ordained by the church (Gal. 3:28; Col. 3:18; 1 Tim. 2:8-15; 3:4-5; 12).

WHAT DOES THE BIBLE SAY ABOUT DIVORCE?

We believe that God hates divorce and intends marriage to last until one of the spouses dies. (Mal. 2).

Divorce and remarriage is regarded as adultery except on the grounds of fornication.

Although divorced and remarried persons or divorced persons may hold positions of service in the church and be greatly used of God for Christian service, they may not be considered for the offices of pastor or deacon (Mal. 2:14-17; Matt. 19:3-12; Rom. 7:1-3; 1 Tim. 3:2, 12. and Titus 1:6).

Does what God says about this subject make any difference? Not only have women pastors totally ignored the basic qualifications set forth in the Bible, many have made a mockery of the moral requirements. Many have engaged in extra-marital affairs; some have been divorced and remarried several times and no one seems to care as long as the women are entertaining and effective (or we should say seductive?).

FOR SERIOUS CONSIDERATION

1. Can you find one example in the Bible of a woman serving as the pastor of a true New-Testament church?

2. Do you believe God has ever called a woman to serve as the pastor of a local church?

3. Where in the Bible do we find God's qualifications of pastor?

4. What does the Bible say about the pastor's married life?

5. How can some of today's popular televangelists continue to get away with their known sexual scandals?

6. Please pray for our churches and our nation.

DEMON DOCTRINES IN THE LAST DAYS

Doctrines of Demons: Read 1 Tim. 3:3-6. 1 *Now the Spirit speaketh expressly, that in the latter times some shall depart from the faith, giving heed to seducing spirits, and **doctrines of devils**; 2 Speaking lies in hypocrisy; having their conscience seared with a hot iron. **3 <u>Forbidding to marry</u>, and commanding to abstain from <u>meats</u>, which God hath created to be received with thanksgiving of them which believe and know the truth.** 4 For every creature of God is good, and nothing to be refused, if it be received with thanksgiving: 5 For it is sanctified by the word of God and prayer. If thou put the brethren in remembrance of these things, thou shalt be a good minister of Jesus Christ. "*

SARDIS

THE DEAD CHURCH

(Rev. 3:1-6) *1 "And to the* **angel of the church in Sardis** *write, 'These things says He who has the seven Spirits of God and the seven stars: "I know your works, that you have a name that you are alive, but you are dead.*

2 Be watchful, and strengthen the things which remain, that are ready to die, for I have not found your works perfect before God.

3 Remember therefore how you have received and heard; hold fast and repent. Therefore if you will not watch, I will come upon you as a thief, and you will not know what hour I will come upon you.

4 You have a few names even in Sardis who have not defiled their garments; and they shall walk with Me in white, for they are worthy.

5 He who overcomes shall be clothed in white garments, and I will not blot out his name from the Book of Life; but I will confess his name before My Father and before His angels.

6 He who has an ear, let him hear what the Spirit says to the churches."

Notice the Change

You will notice a change in the introduction to this church in contrast to the other churches. Up until this point, Christ begins with a commendation of things which the church was doing right. When we come to Sardis, *there is no commendation here on because there was nothing good to commend. Nothing was right.*

Consider the words of G. Campbell Morgan:19 *"There is a marked change in our Lord's method of address to the church at Sardis. Hitherto, He commenced with words of condemnation. Here He commended with words of condemnation. In other churches, evil had not been the habit, but the exception, and therefore it was possible first to commend. Here the case is reversed, and no word of commendation to this church as a church."*

(Psalm 2:8-9) *"Ask of me, and I shall give thee the heathen for thine inheritance, and the uttermost parts of the earth for thy possession. ⁹Thou shalt break them with a rod of iron; thou shalt dash them in pieces like a potter's vessel."*

(Rev. 12:5) *"And she brought forth a man child, who was to rule all nations with a rod of iron."*

(Rev. 19:15)

"And out of his mouth goeth a sharp sword, that with it he should smite the nations: and he shall rule them with a rod of iron: and he treadeth the winepress of the fierceness and wrath of Almighty God."

John Walvoord 20 reminds us that the word "rule"

---

[19]Morgan, G. Campbell, *The Letters of our Lord,* (Westwood, N.J. : Fleming H. Revell Co.) Cited by Walvoord on page 79.
[20]The Revelation of Jesus Christ, Page 76.

(poimanei) literally means to "shepherd." *"That rule will not be simply that of executing judgment, but also that of administering mercy and direction to those who are sheep as contrasted to the goats"* (Matthew 25:31-46).

Is Anybody Listening?

Christ ends this letter with the same admonition He gives to the other churches: "He that hath an ear, let him hear what the Spirit saith unto the churches."

The Depths of Satan

Some members of the congregation had not followed the "depths of Satan." John Walvoord said: *"Here reference is made to the satanic system often seen in great detail in false cults which compete with the true Christian faith. Just as there are the deep things of God (1 Cor. 2:10) which are taught by the Spirit, so there are deep things of Satan which result from his work."*[21]

Doctrines of Demons

The church today should heed this warning. The Holy Spirit warns us that in the latter days, the influence of Satan will be evident in the church. (1 Timothy 4:1). ***"Now the Spirit speaketh expressly, that in the latter times some shall depart from the faith, giving heed to seducing spirits, and doctrines of devils."***

Promise of Millennium

In verses 26-29, God promises something special to those who are faithful. They will have power over the nations and they would rule over the nations with a rod of iron. This is another clear reference to the coming, literal,

---

[21]Walvoord, page 76.

millennial reign of Christ on the earth.

The Seven Spirits of God

What does this mean? I favor the view of commentators like Henry Aflord 22, who believes this is a reference to the Holy Spirit. This view is based on Isaiah 11:2-5, where the Holy Spirit is described as:

1. The Spirit of the Lord

2. The Spirit of Wisdom

3. The Spirit of Understanding

4. The Spirit of Counsel

5. The Spirit of Might,

6. The Spirit of Knowledge

7. The Spirit of the Fear of the Lord.

The Dead Church

The Church at Sardis probably thought they had a great reputation in their city. But in God's eyes, that church was dead. It was all over but the funeral. However, there were a few members who were not dead yet. Those few faithful members were warned *to get their act together* before they too, died.

White Raiment

There were a few faithful people in that church and Christ

---

[22] Henry Alford, *The Greek New Testament*, IV, 579. Cited by Wolvoord in page 79.

encouraged them by promising them two things: They would be clothed in white and their names would not be blotted out of the Book of Life. Some suggest that the white raiment represents festivity, victory, purity, and the heavenly state. In Revelation 19:8, the "fine linen, bright and clean," is clearly the "righteous acts of the saints." This may be hard to believe, but the clothes (wedding garments) we believers will wear to the marriage of Christ and His church will made of our good works. For more information on this, read (2 Cor. 11:2), (Eph. 5:26-27).

The Book of Life (Rev. 3:5)

*He who overcomes shall be clothed in white garments, and **I will not blot out his name from the Book of Life;** but I will confess his name before My Father and before His angels.*

This verse has puzzled expositors. What does this mean? Is this a verse that teaches one can lose his/her salvation? We recommend that each of us study the following questions and read the suggested Scriptures.

1. What is the Book of Life?

(Revelation 20:11-14). *"And I saw a great white throne, and him that sat on it, from whose face the earth and the heaven fled away; and there was found no place for them.*

[12]And I saw the dead, small and great, stand before God; and the books were opened: and another book was opened, which is the book of life: and the dead were judged out of those things which were written in the books, according to their works.

[13]And the sea gave up the dead which were in it; and death and hell delivered up the dead which were in them: and they were judged every man according to their works.

¹⁴*And death and hell were cast into the lake of fire. This is the second death.*¹⁵*And whosoever was not found written in the book of life was cast into the lake of fire."*

2. What is found in the Book of Life?

3. When is a person's name put in the Book of Life?

4. When is a person's name blotted out of the Book of Life?

Is a person's name *blotted out* of the Book of life when they sin? Does that person lose their salvation at that point? Is a person's name blotted out of the Book of life when they die without forgiveness and because they rejected or failed to receive Christ as their personal Savior?

John Walvoord's Explanation

"Some have considered the Book of Life not as the roll of all who are saved but rather a list of all for whom Christ died, that is, all of humanity who have possessed physical life. As they come to maturity, and are faced with the responsibility of accepting or rejecting Christ, their names are blotted out if they fail to receive Christ as Savior; whereas, those who do accept Christ as Savior are confirmed in their position in the Book of Life, and their names are confessed before the Father and the heavenly angels."

Did Jesus die for the world or not?

This present writer has written an article on the subject: *"For Whom Did Christ Die?"* The article is available free of charge to those who desire to do further study on this subject. This article addresses the question of whether Christ died for the whole world or whether he died for a few people called "the Elect." Here are some important Scriptures to consider on this subject:

74

(John 3:16) *"For God so loved **the world,** that he gave his only begotten Son, that **whosoever** believeth in him should not perish, but have everlasting life. For God sent not his Son into **the world** to condemn **the world;** but that **the world** through him might be saved."*

(John 1:29) *"The next day John seeth Jesus coming unto him, and saith, Behold the Lamb of God, which taketh away the sin of the world."*

(1 John 2:2) *"And he is the propitiation for our sins: and not for ours only, but also for the **sins of the whole world.**"*

(Titus 2:11) *"For the grace of God that bringeth salvation hath appeared **to all men.**"*

(1 Tim. 2:4) *"Who will have **all men to be saved**, and to come unto the knowledge of the truth.*

(2 Peter 3:9) *"The Lord is not slack concerning his promise, as some men count slackness; but is longsuffering to us-ward, not willing that **any should perish**, but that **all should come to repentance.**"*

(1 Tim. 2:6) *"Who gave himself a **ransom for all**, to be testified in due time."*

(1 Tim. 4:10) *"For therefore we both labor and suffer reproach, because we trust in the living God, who is **the Savior of all men**, especially of those that believe.*

(2 Peter 2:1) *"But there were false prophets also among the people, even as there shall be false teachers among you, who privately shall bring in damnable heresies, even denying the Lord **that bought them.**"* **We believe Christ died for all sinners and their names are written in the Book of Life. When**

that sinner dies, if he/she has not received Christ as his/her Savior, their names are blotted out of the Book of Life forever.

PHILADELPHIA

THE GOOD CHURCH

(Rev. 3:7-13 *"And to the angel of the church in Philadelphia write; These things saith he that is holy, he that is true, he that hath the key of David, he that openeth, and no man shutteth; and shutteth, and no man openeth;*

[8]I know thy works: behold, I have set before thee an open door, and no man can shut it: for thou hast a little strength, and hast kept my word, and hast not denied my name.

[9]Behold, I will make them of the synagogue of Satan, which say they are Jews, and are not, but do lie; behold, I will make them to come and worship before thy feet, and to know that I have loved thee.

[10]Because thou hast kept the word of my patience, I also will keep thee from the hour of temptation, which shall come upon all the world, to try them that dwell upon the earth.

[11]Behold, I come quickly: hold that fast which thou hast, that no man take thy crown.

[12]Him that overcometh will I make a pillar in the temple of my God, and he shall go no more out: and I will write upon him the name of my God, and the name of the city of my God, which is new Jerusalem, which cometh down out of heaven from my God:

and I will write upon him my new name. [13]He that hath an ear, let him hear what the Spirit saith unto the churches."

The City

This city still exists. Today it is called Alasehir in Turkey. The word *Philadelphia* means brotherly love. In John's day, the city was known for its rich soil and grapes were one of its principal crops. Several times in history, the city was nearly destroyed by earthquakes.

Pagan Religion

Philadelphia, like the other cities of Asia was pagan and Dionysus (also known as Bacchus), the god of wine, was the chief object of worship there. As we noted previously, Bacchus was pictured as the goat-god. The upper part of this idol looked like a man and the lower part looked like a goat with cloven feet and a tail. The picture of Satan with horns etc. did not come from the Bible. It came from the heathen religions of ancient Asia.

No Condemnation

Philadelphia, like Smyrna, are the only two of the seven churches in which Christ did not find anything to condemn. This was a good church.

Christ holds the Keys

Christ reminds them that He holds the keys. Jesus holds the keys to death and hades (Rev. 1:18). Jesus holds the keys to the kingdom (Matt. 16:19). Jesus told this church that He had put an open door before that church that no man (or devil) had the power to shut. When God opens a door, nobody can shut it. When God shuts a door, nobody can open it.

A "little" strength left

Evidently the church had been through great trials, but they had not given up, turned back, or denied their Lord. They were a faithful church. This "little strength" did not suggest they were spiritually weak, but that this was a small church and there were very few believers there.

The hour of "testing"

There is a time of testing coming on this God-hating, Christ-rejecting world. It is called the Great Tribulation (Matthew 24:21). *"For then shall be great tribulation, such as was not since the beginning of the world to this time, no, nor ever shall be."* God protected this church and there have been believers in Philadelphia down through the centuries even under Turkish rule.

John Walvoord reminds us that most of the nominal Christians finally moved to Greece after World War I.

In our opinion, the promise, *"I will keep thee from the hour of temptation,"* can also be interpreted to mean that the church will be kept from (delivered out of) the Great Tribulation that is coming *"to try them that dwell upon the earth."*

As we have previously stated, we believe that chapters 2-3 of The Revelation focus on the Church Age.

We believe the church is taken from the earth in The Revelation, chapter 4 verse 1.

The word church does not appear again because the church is gone (the Rapture).

We believe Chapters 4-19 of The Revelation describe the events which will take place on earth during the Tribulation.

In fact, chapter 6 gives us a complete outline of The Tribulation period.

These same events are found in Matthew 24. We believe Chapters 20-22 of The Revelation focus on the Millennium and the new heaven and the new earth.

The King is coming

One of Christ's last words to this church was a reminder that He is coming back again. And that they should "hang in there." We believe in the imminent return of Jesus Christ. He could return at any time. There will be no warning. All of the signs are fulfilled. We'd better watch and be ready. He could come for His church at any moment.

The Crowns (10-11)

Christ warns them that they should not let anyone take their crown. Their crowns were not salvation. Their crowns were their rewards for faithful service. Salvation cannot be lost but rewards can be lost. For more information on "crowns" you may read: 1 Cor. 9:25, 1 Thess. 2:19, 2 Tim. 4:8, James 1:12, 1 Peter 5:4, Rev. 2:10, Rev. 3;11, Rev.e:4, and Rev. 4:10.

The New Jerusalem (12-13)

The Bible teaches that the New Jerusalem will descend from God out of heaven. This is a literal city described in chapter 21 of The Revelation and we will study it carefully when we reach that chapter.

The heavenly city will not be some *"little cabin in the corner of glory land."* This city will be a cube, 1500 miles long, 1500 miles wide, and 1500 miles high.

This city will be suspended above the earth (like a satellite) during the millennium. In the opinion of this pastor, we saints, who will be in our translated bodies, will be able to travel back and forth from this earth to that city.

This city will be far enough away from the earth so that it will not be effected by the final melt-down (2 Peter 3:10) of the present earth.

2 Peter 3:10-13)

"10 But the day of the Lord will come as a thief in the night; in the which the heavens shall pass away with a great noise, and the elements shall melt with fervent heat, the earth also and the works that are therein shall be burned up.

11Seeing then that all these things shall be dissolved, what manner of persons ought ye to be in all holy conversation and godliness,

12Looking for and hasting unto the coming of the day of God, wherein the heavens being on fire shall be dissolved, and the elements shall melt with fervent heat? 13Nevertheless we, according to his promise, look for new heavens and a new earth, wherein dwelleth righteousness."

The time will come a time when God will erase the memory of this earth, this life, and everything related to it. We will be in a perfect place, with perfect bodies, forever. **(Isaiah 65:17)** *"For, behold, I create new heavens and a new earth: and the former shall not be remembered, nor come into mind."*

References to this City

This is the city Abraham looked for (Hebrews 11:9-16). Vernon McGee wrote that the first floor of this city will be large enough to hold 170 times the present world population.

We recommend that you request a copy of Evangelist Danny Lanier's sermon on heaven. He describes the size of heaven better than anyone we have ever heard. In that message, Danny mentioned things about heaven we had never heard before.

The following information is from Danny's sermon. It is important for you to remember that the statistics you are about to read refer to the new heaven and the new earth described in Revelation 21, *not the present heaven* (paradise) where believers are at the present time.

1,500 square miles

To get an idea of how large the ground floor of heaven is, we could begin at Miami, Florida and draw a line 1,500 miles to the north to the State of Maine. From Maine we would draw the line 1,500 westward to Denver, Colorado. From Denver, we would draw the line south to somewhere in Mexico. Finally, we would draw the line eastward, across the Gulf of Mexico until we reached our point of departure. *That square would be heaven's base.*

528,000 Stories

Heaven is also 1,500 miles high. Our space stations and satellites orbit a mere 250 miles above the earth at 17,000 mph. Heaven's "top floor" will be 1,250 miles higher than our space stations.

We measure the heights of buildings by the number of floors. The World Trade Center had more than 100 floors. If each floor of heaven would have 15 foot ceilings (rather than the normal 8 foot ceilings), heaven would have

528,000 stories and each story would have 2,250,000 square miles (not feet) of space on every floor. That's 1 trillion, 188 billion square miles of space in God's city.

198,000 square miles per person

It is estimated that 30 billion people have been born on earth since creation. If all of them died and went to heaven (which we know they won't), each of them would have 198 square miles of space in heaven.

If only half of the people ever born were saved and went to heaven, they would each have 396,000 square miles of space in heaven.

LAODICEA

THE CHURCH THAT MADE GOD SICK

(Rev. 3:14-19) *14 And unto the angel of the church of the Laodiceans write; These things saith the Amen, the faithful and true witness, the beginning of the creation of God;*

15 I know thy works, that thou art neither cold nor hot: I would thou wert cold or hot.

16 So then because thou art lukewarm, and neither cold nor hot, I will spue thee out of my mouth.

17 Because thou sayest, I am rich, and increased with goods, and have need of nothing; and knowest not that thou art wretched, and miserable, and poor, and blind, and naked:

18 I counsel thee to buy of me gold tried in the fire, that thou mayest be rich; and white raiment, that thou mayest be clothed, and that the shame of thy nakedness do not appear; and anoint thine eyes with eyesalve, that thou mayest see.

19 As many as I love, I rebuke and chasten: be zealous therefore, and repent.

20 Behold, I stand at the door, and knock: if any man hear my voice, and open the door, I will come in to him, and will sup with him, and he with me.

21 To him that overcometh will I grant to sit with me in my throne, even as I also overcame, and am set down with my Father in his throne.

22 He that hath an ear, let him hear what the Spirit saith unto the churches."

Pride Blinds

Someone said that "pride is like a ragged bum walking down the street thinking he is the best-dressed man in town." This church made God sick at His stomach. Yet, they were so proud of themselves.

The City of Laodicea

This city was located about 90 miles due East of Ephesus and under Roman rule it was a very wealthy city. According to Charles Ryie, the city was so wrapped up in material things it did not recognize its true spiritual condition. The city was famous for banking, the production of wool cloth, and medicine. (gold, white garments, and eye salve mentioned in 3:18). Laodicea was also the center for making medicines, including a special tablet that was powdered, mixed with water, and smeared on the eyes. **23**

Beginning of Creation (verse 14): Be very careful here! This does not mean that Christ was "created," or was the first being God created. The idea that Jesus was a created being was one of the first heresies faced by the early church. It was called the "Arian Heresy" named after a heretic named Arius. In A.D. 300, a man named Arius attacked the deity of the Son of God and the Holy Spirit. Arius taught that God the Father created the Son and the

---

[23]*Ryrie Study Bible,* (Chicago: Moody Press, 1995) page 2018.

Son created the Holy Spirit. **This makes them creatures or created beings. This is heresy!**

Jehovah's Witnesses have revived the ancient heresy of Arius. Jehovah's (false) Witnesses make Jesus "a god" rather than the Creator God in John 1:1.**24** According to Jehovah's Witnesses, before Jesus came to earth, he existed as Michael, the Archangel.**25** One former Jehovah's Witness, who had been taught that Jesus was an angel, and a created being, was troubled by reading Hebrews 1: 6-8. No wonder he was troubled!

6 "And again, when he bringeth in the first begotten into the world, he saith, 'And let all the angels of God worship him.'

7 And of the angels he saith, 'Who maketh his angels spirits, and his ministers a flame of fire.'

8 But unto the Son he saith, 'Thy throne, O God, is forever and ever: a scepter of righteousness is the scepter of thy kingdom.'"

This is important! Christ is not the first creation, He is before all creation. In fact, Christ is the Creator! (John 1:1-3) *"In the beginning was the Word, and the Word was with God, and the Word was God. The same was in the beginning with God. All things were made by him; and without him was not anything made that was made."*

---

[24] See The Truth Shall Make You Free, (Brooklyn: Watchtower Bible and Tract Society, 1943) page 47.

[25] Studies in the Scriptures, 5:84.

THREE SPIRITUAL "STATES"

1. Some people are hot toward God. They love God and are "on fire for Him."

2. Others are cold toward God. They are not interested in spiritual things and care nothing for God, church, or the Bible.

3. Others are lukewarm. They have been touched by God; they are probably all church members; some of them are pastors' children who grew up in church; and may probably attended a Christian School. But they have become lukewarm and make God sick at His stomach. This is a pitiful state. God told this church that they would be better off if they were "cold." Why is that?

We have learned that it is much easier to win prostitutes, drug addicts, ex-cons, and others than it is to reach those pitiful, lukewarm people who grew up in church, attended a Christian School, were exposed to the Word of God, and have since lost interest in the things of God and have gone back into the world.

Many of these people seldom attend church, and are living in sin. On the other hand, many of these lukewarm people still attend church, stand behind the pulpits, warm pews, frown through the worship service, and watch the clock during the preaching. This type of person makes God sick at His stomach.

They needed nothing

The pastor and members of the church at Laodecia boasted, *"We are rich and have need of nothing!"* What a joke! Jesus said they were wretched, miserable, poor, blind, and naked." Wow!! Jesus urged that pathetic congregation to real gold (true riches), real clothes, and real medicine (3:17-18). This was a reference to their reputation in banking, production of wool, and the eye-salve they manufactured and sold all over the ancient world, and the famous medical school of Asklepios which was located in Laodecia.

God spanks His children

Christ reminds the church that He chastens (spanks) those he loves. The only way a believer can avoid this "spanking" is to judge himself / herself. **(Hebrews 12:5-9)** *"My son, despise not thou the chastening of the Lord, nor faint when thou art rebuked of him: ⁶For whom the Lord loveth he chasteneth, and scourgeth every son whom he receiveth.*

⁷If ye endure chastening, God dealeth with you as with sons; for what son is he whom the father chasteneth not?

⁸But if ye be without chastisement, whereof all are partakers, ***then are ye bastards, and not sons.***"

(1 Cor. 11:30-32): *"For this cause many are weak and sickly among you, and many sleep. ³¹For if we would **judge ourselves**, we should not be judged. ³²But when we are judged, we are **chastened of the Lord**, that we should not be condemned with the world."*

Christ is outside looking in (Rev. 3:21).

Isn't this sad? Christ loved the church; Christ died for the church; Christ is the head of the church, and here He is on the outside of this church trying to get back in. Evidently, nobody opened the door to let Him in and that church died. There is nothing left of that church today but ruins and weeds.

We will rule with Christ (3:21)

Believers will rule with Christ when he comes to sit on His throne and reign during the Millennium (Revelation 20:4). Is anybody listening?

CHAPTER 4

CROWNS AND THRONES

We believe The Revelation can be understood more clearly by dividing it into three divisions. All three of these divisions are described in Revelation 1:19, where we read: *"Write the things which thou **has seen**, and the things **which are**, and the things **which shall be hereafter**."*

Chapter 1

"Write the things which thou hast seen." The things described in chapter one are past. Those were the things John *had already seen.*

Chapters 2-3

Chapters two and three describe *"The things which are."* We believe these two chapters describe the church age. The Church Age began on the Day of Pentecost, continued during John's day, and continues through the present time. The Church Age will end when Christ returns for His church.

Chapters 4-22

We believe the information found in chapters 4-22 are still future. The last part of Rev. 1:19 concerns *"the things which shall be hereafter."* The words "Shall be" are clearly future. We believe chapter four marks the end of the Church Age. The things which John saw and wrote about in chapters 4-22 are still future.

(Revelation 4:1-11)

"After this I looked, and, behold, a door was opened in heaven: and the first voice which I heard was as it were of a trumpet talking with me; which said, Come up hither, and I will show thee things which must be hereafter.

2And immediately I was in the spirit: and, behold, a throne was set in heaven, and one sat on the throne.

3And he that sat was to look upon like a jasper and a sardine stone: and there was a rainbow round about the throne, in sight like unto an emerald.

4And round about the throne were four and twenty seats: and upon the seats I saw four and twenty elders sitting, clothed in white raiment; and they had on their heads crowns of gold. And out of the throne proceeded lightnings and thunderings and voices: and there were seven lamps of fire burning before the throne, which are the seven Spirits of God.

6And before the throne there was a sea of glass like unto crystal: and in the midst of the throne, and round about the throne, were four beasts full of eyes before and behind.

7And the first beast was like a lion, and the second beast like a calf, and the third beast had a face as a man, and the fourth beast was like a flying eagle.

⁸And the four beasts had each of them six wings about him; and they were full of eyes within: and they rest not day and night, saying, Holy, holy, holy, Lord God Almighty, which was, and is, and is to come.

⁹And when those beasts give glory and honor and thanks to him that sat on the throne, who liveth for ever and ever,

¹⁰The four and twenty elders fall down before him that sat on the throne, and worship him that liveth for ever and ever, and cast their crowns before the throne, saying,

¹¹Thou art worthy, O Lord, to receive glory and honor and power: for thou hast created all things, and for thy pleasure they are and were created."

After This (4:1)

We believe chapter 4, verse 1 marks the end of the church age and the beginning of the things which are to be fulfilled in the future (4-22).

Read verse 1 carefully and then answer the following questions: *"After this I looked, and, behold, a door was opened in heaven: and the first voice which I heard was as it were of a trumpet talking with me; which said, Come up hither, and I will show thee things which must be hereafter."*

1. What does "after this" mean?

2. In which direction did John look?

3. What did John see?

4. Where was the thing John saw?

5. What did the voice tell John to do?

6. What did the Spirit tell John He would show him?

In the opinion of this present writer, the interpretation of this verse is not difficult to understand: John was given of a vision of the past, the present and the future (1-3). When John was taken up into heaven (Rev. 4:1), he was given a vision of things which would take place (in heaven and on earth) at the end of the church age, after Christ removes His church from the earth.

In the Spirit (4:2a)

Verse 2 says that John was "in the spirit." Was John "in the spirit" like Paul was in (2 Corinthians 12:1-4)? Both Paul and John had this experience. Both men saw things human eyes cannot see. The difference between those two experiences is that Paul *was not allowed* to talk about the things he had seen and heard. John *was allowed* to see things and commanded to write about them.

The throne (4:2b)

This is awesome! John was taken to heaven and allowed to actually lay eyes upon the control center of the entire universe. This throne is where God makes decisions and issues orders for angels to carry out. This is the throne where the unsaved dead of all ages will be brought before for their final judgment before being cast into the lake of fire (Revelation 20: 11-14). The appearance of this throne is described in verse 3.

The 24 Elders (4:4)

Who are these people? There are at least three different interpretations of this. Some say they are angels. Others say they represent the saved of all ages. We can't be dogmatic, but in our opinion, we believe they represent the church in heaven. We believe this because of the "clues."

The Crowns

Those 24 elders are wearing crowns. In the Greek language there are two different words for crowns: One type of crown is a *diadem*. The other type of crown is a *stephanos*. A diadem (crown) is a crown worn by a King. A stephanos (crown) is won by a victor. These 24 Elders are wearing stephanos, or victors' crowns. They have won the victory.

Seated With Christ

These 24 Elders, wearing victors' crowns are seated with Christ. This is in harmony with verses like:

(Revelation 3:21). "To him that over-cometh will I grant to sit with me in my throne, even as I also overcame, and am set down with my Father in His throne."

(2 Timothy 2:12) "If we suffer, we shall also reign with him: if we deny him, he also will deny us."

The Seven Spirits of God (4:5)

This is the third[26] reference to the Seven Spirits of God. Who are they? John Walvoord interprets them to be a representation of the Holy Spirit a seven-fold way rather than seven individual spirits.[27] John Walvoord reminds us that the Holy Spirit is invisible unless embodied in some way. For example:

---

[26] Rev. 1:4, Rev. 3:1, & Rev. 4:5
[27] John Walvoord, *The Revelation of Jesus Christ* (Chicago: Moody Press, 1960) pp 107-108.

- The Holy Spirit appeared as a dove at the baptism of Jesus (Matthew 3:13-17).

- The Holy Spirit appeared as cloven tongues of fire on the Day of Pentecost (Acts 2).

- The Holy Spirit also appeared as seven blazing lamps in Revelation 4:5.

- These seven blazing lamps were the means by which John was informed of the presence of the Holy Spirit. *Of unclean lips: for mine eyes have seen the King, the LORD of hosts."*

Four Living Creatures (4:6-9)

No explanation is given for the sea of glass. Some commentators say that "creatures" is a better translation than "beasts." The Greek word for beast is "therion" like the beast coming out of the sea in Revelation 13. The word here is "zoon" which means "living creature." The work of those creatures (created beings) is to continually ascribe holiness to God. These created beings could be angels whose function is to continually bring honor and glory to God. Read about the Cherubim and Seraphim (Isaiah 6:1-5) & (Ezekiel 28:14).

"In the year that king Uzziah died I saw also the Lord sitting upon a throne, high and lifted up, and his train filled the temple.

2Above it stood the seraphims: each one had six wings; with twain he covered his face, and with twain he covered his feet, and with twain he did fly.

3And one cried unto another, and said, Holy, holy, holy, is the LORD of hosts: the whole earth is full of his glory.

4And the posts of the door moved at the voice of him that cried, and the house was filled with smoke.

5Then said I, Woe is me! For I am undone; because I am a man of unclean lips, and I dwell in the midst of a people

The Order of Created Beings

It may be important at this point to remember the order of beings in the universe God created.

- The Cherubim and the Seraphim
- Angels
- Man
- Animals

Notice the order in which Israel camped

John Walvoord28 quotes Walter Scott in reminding us that these animals also represent the way the tribes of Israel pitched their tents and raised their standards as they camped on the four sides around the Tabernacle in the wilderness.

- The emblem of the tribe of Judah was a *Lion.*
- The emblem of the tribe of Ephraim was an *ox.*
- The emblem of the tribe of Reuben was a *man.*
- The emblem of the tribe of Dan was an eagle.

Aspects of Divine Majesty

We believe John Walvoord has the best interpretation. He wrote: "All of these creatures are supreme in their respective categories.

---

[28]Walvoord, page 110.

- The lion is king of the beasts and represents majesty and omnipotence;

- The calf or ox represents the most important of domestic animals and signifies patience and continuous labor;

- Man is the greatest of all God's creatures, especially in intelligence and national power;

- And the eagle is greatest among birds and is symbolic of sovereignty and supremacy."29

Casting Crowns (4:10)

As we stated previously, these people are the saved people from the church age who have already died, have been raised (or translated if they were alive when Christ returned for His church), judged, and rewarded. They are wearing victors' crowns (stephanos, not diadems). These crowns are the rewards for faithful service they rendered to Christ while they were alive on the earth. Jesus told us that those who were faithful would receive a "crown" of life. Salvation is a free gift, but rewards (crowns) were awarded for faithful service.

Five Crowns available to Believers

There are at least five (5) crowns available to believers for their faithful service to our Lord.   It is also important to mention at this point that although salvation cannot be lost.

Crowns *can be lost* **or** *not earned* **at all**.   For a better understanding of these "crowns," read: (1 Cor. 9:25, (1

29Walvoord, page 110

Thess. 2:19), (2 Tim. 4:8), (James 1:12), (1 Peter 5:4), (Rev. 2:10), (Rev. 3;11), (Rev. 4:4), and (Rev. 4:10). In this vision, these people cast their crowns at the feet of Jesus. *This is an awesome sight.*

1. Crowns are Rewards for Faithful Service (1 Cor. 9:24-27)

24 "Know ye not that they which run in a race run all, but one receiveth the prize? So run, that ye may obtain.

25 And every man that striveth for the mastery is temperate in all things. Now they do it to obtain a corruptible crown; but we an incorruptible.

26 I therefore so run, not as uncertainly; so fight I, not as one that beateth the air:

27 But I keep under my body, and bring it into subjection: lest that by any means, when I have preached to others, I myself should be a castaway."

2. Crowns (rewards) Can be Lost (Revelation 2:11)
"Behold, I come quickly: hold that fast which thou hast, that no man take thy crown."

3. We will have these crowns on our heads when first arrive in heaven (Rev. 4:4). *"And round about the throne were four and twenty seats: and upon the seats I saw four and twenty elders sitting, clothed in white raiment; and they had on their heads crowns of gold. "*

4. We will cast these crowns at the feet of Jesus (Rev. 4:10). *"The four and twenty elders fall down before him that sat on the throne, and worship him that liveth for ever and ever, and cast their crowns before the throne, saying, ¹¹Thou art worthy, O*

Lord, to receive glory and honor and power: for thou hast created all things, and for thy pleasure they are and were created."

FIVE CROWNS WE COULD WIN

1. (James 1:12) A Reward for not giving in to temptation (The Crown of Life) *"Blessed is the man that endureth temptation: for when he is tried, he shall receive the crown of life, which the Lord hath promised to them that love him."*

2. (1 Thess. 2:19-20) The Soul Winner's Crown (The Crown of Rejoicing) *"For what is our hope, or joy, or crown of rejoicing? Are not even ye in the presence of our Lord Jesus Christ at his coming? [20]For ye are our glory and joy."*

3. (2 Tim. 4:8) A reward for Fighting a Good Fight and Keeping the Faith (Crown of Righteousness) *"I have fought a good fight, I have finished my course, I have kept the faith: [8]Henceforth there is laid up for me a crown of righteousness, which the Lord, the righteous judge, shall give me at that day: and not to me only, but unto all them also that love his appearing."*

4. (1 Peter 5:1-4) A Reward for Faithful Pastors (The Crown of Glory) *"The elders which are among you I exhort, who am also an elder, and an witness of the sufferings of Christ, and also a partaker of the glory that shall be revealed:*

[2]Feed the flock of God which is among you, taking the oversight thereof, not by constraint, but willingly; not for filthy lucre, but of a ready mind;

[3]*Neither as being lords over God's heritage, but being ensamples to the flock.*

[4]And when the chief Shepherd shall appear, ye shall receive a crown of glory that fadeth not away."

5. (Rev. 2:10) To those who are faithful unto death (a Crown of Life) *"Fear none of those things which thou shalt suffer: behold, the devil shall cast some of you into prison, that ye may be tried; and ye shall have tribulation ten days: be thou faithful unto death, and I will give thee a crown of life."*

.

CHAPTER 5

THE SCROLLS AND THE SEALS

1 *"And I saw in the right hand of him that sat on the throne a book written within and on the backside, sealed with seven seals.*

²And I saw a strong angel proclaiming with a loud voice, Who is worthy to open the book, and to loose the seals thereof?

³And no man in heaven, nor in earth, neither under the earth, was able to open the book, neither to look thereon.

⁴And I wept much, because no man was found worthy to open and to read the book, neither to look thereon.

⁵And one of the elders saith unto me, Weep not: behold, the Lion of the tribe of Judah, the Root of David, hath prevailed to open the book, and to loose the seven seals thereof.

⁶And I beheld, and, lo, in the midst of the throne and of the four beasts, and in the midst of the elders, stood a Lamb as it had been slain, having seven horns and seven eyes, which are the seven Spirits of God sent forth into all the earth.

⁷And he came and took the book out of the right hand of him that sat upon the throne.

8And when he had taken the book, the four beasts and four and twenty elders fell down before the Lamb, having every one of them harps, and golden vials full of odours, which are the prayers of saints.

9And they sung a new song, saying, Thou art worthy to take the book, and to open the seals thereof: for thou wast slain, and hast redeemed us to God by thy blood out of every kindred, and tongue, and people, and nation;

10And hast made us unto our God kings and priests: and we shall reign on the earth.

11And I beheld, and I heard the voice of many angels round about the throne and the beasts and the elders: and the number of them was ten thousand times ten thousand, and thousands of thousands;

12Saying with a loud voice, Worthy is the Lamb that was slain to receive power, and riches, and wisdom, and strength, and honour, and glory, and blessing.

13And every creature which is in heaven, and on the earth, and under the earth, and such as are in the sea, and all that are in them, heard I saying, Blessing, and honor, and glory, and power, be unto him that sitteth upon the throne, and unto the Lamb for ever and ever.

14And the four beasts said, Amen. And the four and twenty elders fell down and worshiped him that liveth for ever and ever."

The Scroll with the 7 Seals

This scroll is the scroll that contains the prophecy of impending events that are about to unfold on the earth. This scroll will give us a "sneak preview" of the entire Tribulation Period.

The Strong Angel

There are two references to this strong angel (Revelation 10:1 and Revelation 18:21).

(Rev. 10:1) *"And I saw another mighty angel come down from heaven, clothed with a cloud: and a rainbow was upon his head, and his face was as it were the sun, and his feet as pillars of fire."*

(Rev. 18:21) *"And a mighty angel took up a stone like a great millstone, and cast it into the sea, saying, Thus with violence shall that great city Babylon be thrown down, and shall be found no more at all."*

Who is this strong angel? In the opinion of this present writer, this is probably Gabriel, who told Daniel to seal up the information in his prophecy in Daniel 12:4 and 12:9.

(Daniel 12:4) *"But thou, O Daniel, shut up the words, and seal the book, even to the time of the end: many shall run to and fro, and knowledge shall be increased."*

(Daniel 12:9) *"And he said, Go thy way, Daniel: for the words are closed up and sealed till the time of the end."*

The only Person worthy to open the Seals

Jesus is the only person in the universe who is worthy to open the scroll which contains the judgments that are about to be unleashed upon the earth. **Jesus is pictured two ways in the Bible.** He is portrayed as a lamb and he is portrayed as a lion. The first time Jesus came, he came as a lamb, to die for the sins of the world. When Jesus returns, He will come as a lion to bring judgment upon the earth. As the lamb, Jesus came in meekness and is judged and crucified by sinful men.

The Lion of Judah

Jesus is referred to as *"The Lion of the tribe of Judah"* in (Genesis 49:9-10). *"Judah is a lion's whelp: from the prey, my son, thou art gone up: he stooped down, he couched as a lion, and as an old lion; who shall rouse him up? ¹⁰The sceptre shall not depart from Judah, nor a lawgiver from between his feet, until Shiloh come; and unto him shall the gathering of the people be."*

Vernon McGee Wrote

*"The **LAMB** character refers to His **FIRST** coming, for a lamb speaks of His meekness. As a lamb, He is our Savior; as a lamb, He is judged; The lamb speaks of the Grace of God. The **LION** character refers to His **SECOND** coming, since the lion speaks of His majesty. As a lion, He is sovereign; as a lion, He is judge; The lion speaks of the government of God."*

Jesus Opened the Scroll

This takes place just before the Tribulation. Here is when Jesus will take the scroll (Rev. 5:7) and begin to pour out His wrath upon a sin-loving, God-hating, Christ-rejecting world. Remember, all judgment has been turned over to the Son (Jesus).

(Daniel 7:13-14) *"I saw in the night visions, and, behold, one like the Son of man came with the clouds of heaven, and came to the Ancient of days, and they brought him near before him.*

14And there was given him dominion, and glory, and a kingdom, that all people, nations, and languages, should serve him: his dominion is an everlasting dominion, which shall not pass away, and his kingdom that which shall not be destroyed."

(John 5:22-23) *"For the Father judgeth no man, but hath committed all judgment unto the Son: 23That all men should honor the Son, even as they honor the Father. He that honoreth not the Son honoreth not the Father which hath sent him."*

Jesus is Worshiped (Rev. 5:7-10)

At this point, the Elders and the living creatures break out in songs of praise to Jesus, who is worthy to open the seals. The text says they sang a *NEW SONG!* Notice what happened next. When the Elders and living creatures begin to sing this new song, they are joined by millions of angels.

- **Question: What did these angels do?**

- **Did the angels sing?**

- **Did you know that there is not one verse in the entire Bible that says angels sing?**

- **Angels always "SAY." Angels NEVER sing**!

(Rev. 5:12-13) *Saying a loud voice, Worthy is the Lamb that was slain to receive power, and riches, and wisdom, and strength, and honor, and glory, and blessing.*

*13And every creature which is in heaven, and on the earth, and under the earth, and such as are in the sea, and all that are in them, heard I **saying**, Blessing, and honor, and glory, and power, be unto him that sitteth upon the throne, and unto the Lamb for ever and ever.*

[14]*And the **four beasts said,** Amen. And the four and twenty elders fell down and worshiped him that liveth for ever and ever."*

CHAPTER 6

A PREVIEW OF THE TRIBULATION

In our opinion, Chapter Six of The Revelation provides us with an outline of the events that will take place on the earth during the Tribulation.

We believe the church is raptured in Chapter four, verse one. John sees the sealed book in the hand of Christ in Chapter Five, and the events of the Tribulation begin to move rapidly when we come to Chapter Six.

We also believe that the events in Chapter Six of The Revelation correspond perfectly with the things predicted by Jesus in Matthew 24: 5-8. We believe these events are literal and future.

John Walvoord,30 John Walvoord, who is a Pre-millennialist, places this in the Tribulation period. The church has been Raptured and these are literal events that will take place during the Tribulation.

---

[30]John Walvoord, The Revelation of Jesus Christ, (Chicago: Moody Press, 1966)

Ray Summers,31 who is an Amillennialist, rejects the literal approach to The Revelation. He also rejects the Rapture, the Tribulation, and the Millennium. Like all who try to "spiritualize" the Word of God, Summers tries to make this chapter "fit" somewhere in past history.

Loraine Boettner 32, who is a Post-millennialist, does not attempt to interpret this at all. He dismisses the whole Pre-millennial position and spends most of his time trying to justify his position.

SUMMARY OF CHAPTER SIX

The six Seals in chapter six of The Revelation provide us with a complete picture of the Tribulation period, beginning with the appearance of Anti-Christ and his platform of peace (white horse) and ending with the final judgments of God upon the earth (sixth seal).

The Trumpet and Vial (bowl) judgments that follow in chapters eight and nine clarify and amplify these same judgments.

The Tribulation actually begins when the church is caught up in chapter four, verse one, but the world at large will not realize it. After all, the National Council of Churches will still be here; Many Catholic Priests, Bishops, and Popes will still be here; all lost/Liberal Theologians and religious leaders will still be here, and they no doubt issue some official statement to the press that will account for all of the missing persons.

---

[31] Ray Summers, Worthy is the Lamb, (Nashville: Broadman Press, 1951)

[32] Loraine Boettner, The Millennium (Philadelphia: The Presbyterian and Reformed Publishing Company)

1. The False Christ

When the man on the white horse appears during the Tribulation, the situation will begin to change quickly. Some (Muslims) will believe that he is the Muslim Mahdi and many will be led to believe the Millennium has come. His platform will be "peace on earth" and the nations will be relieved and will welcome this imposter on the white horse with open arms. This period of peace will be short lived. When the rider on the red horse appears, Revelation 6:4 says that peace will be taken from the earth and you will notice that he has a large sword. This comes at a time when the world is beginning to enjoy their period of peace on earth. It is at this point that skirmishes begin to erupt between nations and soon war will break out and this conflict will engulf the whole world.

2. War & Famine

Just as night follows day, famine will follow these wars. The wars are world-wide and so will be the famine. During those days it will take a days' wage to feed a family of two even if they eat horse food (barley).33

3. Death and Hell

Just as certainly as famine follows war, death will follow this world-wide famine.34 The devastation of this famine will be unprecedented. One-fourth of the entire earth's population will die from this famine, disease, and pestilence.

---

[33] See Rev. 6:6
[34] Revelation 6:6-7

4. Man-eating Beast

To make matters worse, many people will be killed and eaten by the starving beasts that will roam the earth during this period.

5. Judgment

When we come to the sixth seal (Revelation 6:9-11), the scene shifts briefly from earth to heaven. In this vision, John saw the souls of the Tribulation martyrs, under the alter in heaven.

It may well be that everybody saved during the Tribulation will suffer martyrdom. The individuals in this scene are dead but they have not been resurrected yet. They are still in their temporary bodies awaiting the end of the Tribulation, the martyrdom of the rest of those who will be killed, and the just judgment of God upon their murderers upon the earth.

Some have objected to their plea for revenge upon their tormentors on earth. Their cry for righteous judgment is in the same spirit as the Psalmists call to God to vindicate His holiness and righteousness in dealing with the injustice and oppression which characterizes the human race." 35

6. The climax

The final scene in the Sixth Seal is the climax and consummation of the judgments of the Tribulation. The Seals are a complete outline and summary of the final judgments.

---

[35] John Walvoord, The Revelation of Jesus Christ, (Chicago: Moody Press, 19??) P 134.

- The Trumpets and Bowls (vials) all amplify and clarify these final judgments.

- The Seventh Seal is amplified in the Trumpets, and

- The Seventh Trumpet is amplified in the Bowls (vials).

Vernon McGee made a very interesting observation. He wrote: *"We have seen the riding of the four horsemen and this follows exactly the same pattern the Lord Jesus gave while he was on the earth. In Matthew 24:5-8, He said, 'For many will come in my name, saying I am Christ, and shall deceive many* **(White Horse).** *"And when you shall hear of wars and rumors of wars* **(Red Horse);** *see that you be not troubled, for all these things must come to pass, but the end is not yet. For nation shall rise up against nation, and kingdom; and there shall be famines"* **(Black Horse),** *and pestilence* **(Pale Horse),** *and earthquakes in divers places. All these are the beginning of sorrows.' "*36 **All of this is the opening of the period called the Tribulation.**

1. The White Horse (6:2) *"And I saw, and behold a white horse: and he that sat on him had a bow; and a crown was given unto him: and he went forth conquering, and to conquer."*

In our opinion, the man on the white horse is the Anti-Christ. He comes on the scene on the white horse in order to deceive the nations. His platform is "peace on earth." This man (perhaps the Mahdi the Muslims are looking for) will deceive the nations and for a brief period, there will actually be peace on earth.

Walvoord says that the rider on the white horse is *the Prince that shall come* mentioned in Daniel 9:26. This person

---

36Vernon McGee, <u>Thru the Bible Commentary</u>, (Nashville: Thomas Nelson, 1983) p 945.

will be the head of the revived Roman Empire and ultimately will become the world ruler. This man is Satan's mouthpiece and the counterfeit of all that Christ is or claims to be. He is therefore cast in the role of conqueror, which seems to be the significance of the white horse. 37

Summers says this is all pantomime. He identifies the rider on the White Horse as the Parthians who would eventually conquer Rome. This of course, is supposed to encourage suffering Christians. 38

Richardson: Summers also quotes Richardson who identifies the rider on the White Horse as Christ, or perhaps the cause of Christ and the progress of the Gospel.39

2. The Red Horse: War (6:3-4)

3And when he had opened the second seal, I heard the second beast say, Come and see. 4And there went out another horse that was red: and power was given to him that sat thereon to take peace from the earth, and that they should kill one another: and there was given unto him a great sword.

The Red Horse symbolizes the war that will break out after the brief period of peace under the Anti-Christ. This rider has a large sword and has the power to take peace from the earth. In just a short time, open warfare will soon engulf the whole world.

- **According to Walvoord,** there will be a series of wars, the greatest of which will be under way at the time of Christ's Second Coming. 40

---

[37] Walvoord, page 126
[38] Summers, page 141, 139
[39] Summers, pages 139-140
[40]Walvoord, page 129

- **Summers** believes this is more pageantry.41

- **Gromacki** believes the Red Horse of the Second Seal pictures war, civil anarchy, and bloodshed.42

3. The Black Horse: Famine (Rev. 6:5-6)

5And when he had opened the third seal, I heard the third beast say, Come and see. And I beheld, and lo a black horse; and he that sat on him had a pair of balances in his hand. 6And I heard a voice in the midst of the four beasts say, A measure of wheat for a penny, and three measures of barley for a penny; and see thou hurt not the oil and the wine."

Just as night follows day, famine follows war. This war will be world-wide and so will be the famine. In those days, it will take a full days wage to purchase enough food for an individual or a small family to survive. The famine will wipe out the food supply and the economy will be in shambles.

Walvoord reminds us that the coin designated as the "penny" is actually a Roman denarius, which is worth about 15 cents. In the wage scale of that time, it was common for a person to receive a denarius for an entire days' labor. A measure of wheat is approximately what a laboring man would eat in one meal. If he used his penny to buy barley, a cheaper food (horse food), one days' labor could buy enough for three good meals. If he chose to eat wheat, his days' labor would buy one meal. 43

Summers, following the Amillennial **line** says that famine always follows in the wake of war and that war, military

---

[41]Summers, page 141

[42]Robert Gramacki, New Testament Survey (Grand Rapids: Baker Publishing House, 1974) page 405

[43] Walvoord, page 123

power, famine, and pestilence are all forces God can use to destroy the oppressors of God's people. Christians are supposed to be encouraged by all of this.44

4. The Pale Horse: Death and Hell (6:7-8)

7And when he had opened the fourth seal, I heard the voice of the fourth beast say, Come and see.

8And I looked, and behold a pale horse: and his name that sat on him was Death, and Hell followed with him. And power was given unto them over the fourth part of the earth, to kill with sword, and with hunger, and with death, and with the beasts of the earth.

Food Shortage

We believe it is inevitable that with the whole world at war and experiencing a food shortage, many people will die. During this period alone, one-fourth of the world's population will die.

Wild Animals

It is interesting to notice also that along with this shortage of food, there will be a population explosion among the animal kingdom. These wild beasts will roam the earth looking for food.

It is reasonable to assume that, having tasted the human flesh of the dead bodies of those who die in the wars and famine. They will then begin to stalk and attack the living and eat them too.

Walvoord says that if one fourth of the world's population is destroyed, it would represent the greatest destruction of

---

44 Summers, page 142

human life ever recorded in history. If treated geographically, it would be equivalent to the destruction of more than the entire population of Europe and South America.45

Summers has nothing to offer here since he, like all Amillennialist, view this as pageantry. He says, "This judgment is only partial; it touches only a fourth part of the earth."46 Summers interprets this to be just some of the forces God will use to destroy the Roman Empire so that God's people will cease to be oppressed.

Martyred Saints (6:9-11)

"9And when he had opened the fifth seal, I saw under the altar the souls of them that were slain for the word of God, and for the testimony which they held:

10And they cried with a loud voice, saying, How long, O Lord, holy and true, dost thou not judge and avenge our blood on them that dwell on the earth?

11And white robes were given unto every one of them; and it was said unto them, that they should rest yet for a little season, until their fellow-servants also and their brethren, that should be killed as they were, should be fulfilled."

Tribulation Martyrs

In this scene, we believe the action shifts from earth to heaven where we see the souls of the Tribulation martyrs under the Alter in heaven. These are men and woman who died for their faith during the Tribulation and are pleading with God to judge their persecutors on earth, who are still

---

[45] Walvoord, page 131
[46]Summers, page 142

living and killing believers. These people are dead but they have not been resurrected yet. This also means that they were not part of the church because the church has already been Raptured and the "dead in Christ" who were raised from their graves and given resurrection bodies at the Rapture.

John Walvoord, a Premillennialist, agrees with this.47

Vernon McGee believes these are both the Old Testament Saints and those who have been killed during the Tribulation.48

Charles Ryrie believes these are the martyrs of the first months of the Tribulation period.

Ray Summers believed that these can be none other than the martyrs of the Domitianic persecution.49

Loraine Boettner (Reform theology) exposes his position regarding the book of The Revelation by saying: *On the other hand, we believe that the principle of literal interpretation which characterizes all types of Pre-millennialism leads to serious error."*50

God's Wrath (6:12-17)

"12And I beheld when he had opened the sixth seal, and, lo, there was a great earthquake; and the sun became black as sackcloth of hair, and the moon became as blood;

13And the stars of heaven fell unto the earth, even as a fig tree casteth her untimely figs, when she is shaken of a mighty wind.

---

[47]Walvoord, page 133
[48]Vernon McGee, Vol. V, page 945
[49]Summers, page 142
[50]Boettner, page 374

14And the heaven departed as a scroll when it is rolled together; and every mountain and island were moved out of their places.

15And the kings of the earth, and the great men, and the rich men, and the chief captains, and the mighty men, and every bondman, and every free man, hid themselves in the dens and in the rocks of the mountains;

16And said to the mountains and rocks, Fall on us, and hide us from the face of him that sitteth on the throne, and from the wrath of the Lamb:

17For the great day of his wrath is come; and who shall be able to stand?"

We believe this seal gives the reader a glimpse of the judgments that will come from God during the last half of the Tribulation period. There is a tendency among scholars to avoid taking these things literally. These are literal judgments that are coming on the earth. Before the Tribulation is over, the entire universe will be affected.

- The earthquake is real.
- The sun will literally become black.
- The moon will literally become red.
- The stars will literally fall from heaven.
- Men will literally try to hide from God.

At this point in history, time has run out for this sin-loving, God-hating, Christ-rejecting world. Divine judgment has finally come. It's "payday" for the inhabitants of the earth.

Walvoord believes that beginning with the Sixth Seal, God is undertaking a direct intervention in human affairs. The judgments of war, famine, death, and the martyrdom of the saints have largely originated in human decision and in the evil heart of man. The judgment described here, however, originates in God as a divine punishment inflicted upon a blasphemous world. 51

Ray Summers, the Amillennialist, says there are two views about this symbolism. One group, he says, holds that this does not represent the final judgment, but only a temporal judgment by natural calamity. The other group holds that this is symbolic of the final judgment. 52

Prophecy Update (2007)

Do you remember recently when your pastor preached about the President of Iran? We spoke of him on March 26, 2006 and quoted from an article titled "Mushrooming Crisis." The timely article revealed that this man was not only developing nuclear weapons, he was boasting openly about blowing Israel off of the map of the earth. There was something else in that article that grabbed our attention. He stated that he believed his mission in life was to prepare the way for the coming of the Muslim Mahdi.

Osama Bin Laden

According to G2 Bulletins [53] military sources, some of the detainees held at Guantanamo Bay have told interrogators *they joined Bin Laden's Al-Qaeda offensive because they thought he was the awaited "enlightened one."* It was also reported that some of the terrorists crossing the border into Iraq were *doing so because of their belief in this Islamic prophecy."*

---

[51]Walvoord, page 136
[52] Summers, page 143, 144
[53]World Net Daily (Sept 8, 2003)

The Muslim Mahdi

Muslims are looking for the appearance of a person they call the "Mahdi" or the "Twelfth Imam. Muslims believe this man is the man riding the white horse in Revelation 6. I am inclined to agree. According to Muslims, this Mahdi was born in 869 and did not die but rather was hidden by God. This is referred to as the Occultation.

Muslims believe the Mahdi will later emerge with Jesus in order to fulfill their mission of bringing peace and justice to the world. **They believe the Mahdi and Jesus will kill all Jews and Christians** and bring "peace" on earth by uniting the whole world in the worship Allah. There are several videos on Youtube on this subject. We'd better take this seriously.

The scene is set and the world is ready

The groundwork for this godless, one world system is already underway among the nations of the world. The Bible calls this the "Mystery of iniquity." Read 2 Thess. 2 again with this in mind.

CHAPTER 7

THE 144,000 AND THE GREAT MULTITUDE

Chapter seven of The Revelation provides additional details of the events that will transpire during the Great Tribulation following the Rapture of the church.

70th Week of Daniel

This chapter (chapter 7) deals with the same events which are mentioned in the 70th week of Daniel (Daniel 9:26). We believe these events are both literal and future.

Two Groups

The focus of this chapter is on two different groups of people who will play an important role on earth during this period. The first group is the 144,000 (Rev. 7:3-8) who are "sealed." The second group is the great multitude that no one could number "from all nations, tribes, peoples, and tongues" (Rev. 7:9-17). Nearly all scholars agree that the "sealing" in this chapter is a symbol of protection, but "when an attempt to identify these two groups mentioned, there is wide disagreement."[54]

---

[54]Ray Summers, Worthy is the lamb, (Nashville: Broadman Press,

Pre-Millennialist, who take the Bible literally, identify the 144,000 as Jews who are sealed for protection during the "Time of Jacob's Trouble," [55] and the great multitude are Gentiles from all nations who are saved during the Tribulation. This is the clear, plain, and obvious meaning of this chapter.

A-Millennialist, on the other hand, and others who revert to the allegorical method of interpretation of Origen and Augustine, can never agree on what anything means. The only thing they can agree on is that The Revelation should not be taken literally.

In our personal opinion, their position (Amillennialist) is not based on legitimate exegesis and sound hermaneutical principles, but rather theological bias. Their entire approach stems from their adamant hatred of the concept of a literal Kingdom of God on this earth as taught in Revelation 20.

The sealing of the 144,000 (Rev. 7:1-8)

When does this take place? Where does this take place? Who are these people? What is the significance of the sealing? What is their ministry during the Tribulation? *"And after these things I saw four angels standing on the four corners of the earth, holding the four winds of the earth, that the wind should not blow on the earth, nor on the sea, nor on any tree.*

²And I saw another angel ascending from the east, having the seal of the living God: and he cried with a loud voice to the four angels, to whom it was given to hurt the earth and the sea,

---

1951) p 146.
[55] Jacob is another name for Israel.

3Saying, Hurt not the earth, neither the sea, nor the trees, till we have sealed the servants of our God in their foreheads.

4And I heard the number of them which were sealed: and there were sealed an hundred and forty and four thousand of all the tribes of the children of Israel.

5Of the tribe of Judah were sealed twelve thousand. Of the tribe of Reuben were sealed twelve thousand. Of the tribe of Gad were sealed twelve thousand.

6Of the tribe of Aser were sealed twelve thousand. Of the tribe of Nepthalim were sealed twelve thousand. Of the tribe of Manasses were sealed twelve thousand.

7Of the tribe of Simeon were sealed twelve thousand. Of the tribe of Levi were sealed twelve thousand. Of the tribe of Issachar were sealed twelve thousand. Of the tribe of Zabulon were sealed twelve thousand. Of the tribe of Joseph were sealed twelve thousand. Of the tribe of Benjamin were sealed twelve thousand.

The Sealing of the Great Multitude (Rev. 7:9-17)

When does this take place? Who are these people? Where are these people? Why are they there? How did they get there? What is the significance of the robes and their crowns? What is their privilege there?

9After this I beheld, and, lo, a great multitude, which no man could number, of all nations, and kindreds, and people, and tongues, stood before the throne, and before the Lamb, clothed with white robes, and palms in their hands;

10And cried with a loud voice, saying, Salvation to our God which sitteth upon the throne, and unto the Lamb.

11And all the angels stood round about the throne, and about the elders and the four beasts, and fell before the throne on their

125

faces, and worshipped God, Saying, Amen: Blessing, and glory, and wisdom, and thanksgiving, and honor, and power, and might, be unto our God for ever and ever. Amen.

[13]And one of the elders answered, saying unto me, What are these which are arrayed in white robes? and whence came they?

[14]And I said unto him, Sir, thou knowest. And he said to me, These are they which came out of great tribulation, and have washed their robes, and made them white in the blood of the Lamb.

[15]Therefore are they before the throne of God, and serve him day and night in his temple: and he that sitteth on the throne shall dwell among them.

[16]They shall hunger no more, neither thirst any more; neither shall the sun light on them, nor any heat. [17]For the Lamb which is in the midst of the throne shall feed them, and shall lead them unto living fountains of waters: and God shall wipe away all tears from their eyes."

Common Questions

It is common for people who reject the idea of a Rapture and a literal Kingdom to ask how anybody can be saved after the Rapture of the Church if the Holy Spirit is gone?

It is true that the Holy Spirit dwells in believers and the Holy Spirit is clearly the one who is restraining the "Man of Sin" (2 Thes. 2).

They reason, that when believers leave the earth, the Holy Spirit will leave as well. In the opinion of this present writer, the Holy Spirit will definitely have a ministry during the Tribulation just like He has in every age. The difference is, The ministry of the Holy Spirit will be different from what it is today in the Church Age.

- **The Restrainer Removed**: For one thing, He (the Holy Spirit) will *no longer restrain sin*. He will *allow* the Man of Sin to appear and go about His work without restraint.

- **Like the Old Testament:** Another opinion is that the work of the Holy Spirit during the Tribulation will be similar to His work in the Old Testament. He dealt with Israel in the Old Testament and He will deal with Israel again during the Tribulation. We will see in a moment, what the work of the Holy Spirit will be in the lives of these two groups of people mentioned in chapter seven.

Our Interpretation of Chapter 7

In the opinion of this present writer, this chapter describes events that will take place during the Tribulation. The events here are both literal an future. This is the same period described in Daniel 9:26. The Tribulation period is also referred to as the "70th week of Daniel," and the "Time of Jacob's Trouble."

- **Four Angels**: The chapter begins with four angels holding the winds (of judgment) back until the 144,000 are sealed (Rev. 7;1-3). Angels are created beings. God created angels *to minister to the heirs of salvation*.[56] Isn't it reasonable to assume that these two groups mentioned in this chapter are "heirs" (going to receive) salvation?

- **Sealed For Protection**: God has often sealed certain people to protect them from judgment and/or harm.

---

[56] Hebrews 1:14

- **God protected Noah** when He sent the flood to destroy the earth and every living thing.

- **God protected Rahab the harlot** when He sent Joshua to destroy the city of Jericho.

- **God protected Lot** when He sent the angels to destroy the cities of Sodom and Gomorrah.

- **God is sealing these people for protection** during this dreadful period coming on the earth.

Walvoord (Premillennial): John Walvoord agrees that these events take place during the Tribulation.[57]

Summers (Amillennial): Ray Summers evidently is a preterist (past) and seeks to find most of The Revelation fulfilled in the days of the persecution under the Roman Emperor Domition.[58] Summers wrote: *"All scholars appear to recognize that this sealing is for protection. The language is similar to that of Ezekiel 9:1 where a mark is placed upon the forehead of God's people, and the agents of destruction are forbidden to touch every person who is thus marked."*[59]

The 144,000 Sealed

This is a literal number. In this chapter, God seals 144,000 people. These are literal people and the number is literal. God seals them to protect them from the horrible judgments which are about to fall on the earth.

---

[57] John Wolvoord, The Revelation of Jesus Christ (Chicago: Moody Press, 1966) pages 20-23.
[58] Ray Summers, Worthy is the Lamb, (Nashville: Broadman, 1951) pages 33-34 & 43-44.
[59]

They are all Jews: Who are these people? Are they Jehovah's Witnesses? Are they the church? Are they some "Spiritual Israel?" Are they Gentiles? Are they citizens from Great Britain?[60] The Holy Spirit makes it clear that these people are from the children of Israel. These people are all Jews. Not only are they Jews, they are all virgins. We are even told what tribes they come from.

The Tribes are not lost

Someone will often raise the objection that ten of the tribes of Israel are "lost." In our opinion, the tribes may have been lost to historians, but they've never been lost to God. He knows right where they are. In fact, to whom did James address his letter? Was it not the twelve tribes which were scattered? **(James 1:1)** *"James, a servant of God and of the Lord Jesus Christ, **to the twelve tribes which are scattered abroad**, greeting."*

Summers: "Twelve is the symbolic number for organized religion and is meant to convey the idea of an immense number."[61] Summers quotes five authors who reject the literal interpretation. [62]

Pieters: "The church militant and the church triumphant."

Richardson: "There is no distinction between Jew and Gentile."

D. Smith: "These are the true Israel, the Israel of God (Galatians 6:16).

---

[60] *British Israelism* is a popular doctrine.
[61] Summers, page 46
[62] Summers, pages 147-148

Swete: "The whole church. The same body under widely different conditions."

Beckwith: "The whole body of the church. . . . Jew and Gentiles alike."

The Difference between Israel and the Church

It is important to stress at this point that much confusion has been caused by ignoring the distinctions between Israel and the church. Nearly all of the "weird interpretations" of The Revelation, view the church and Israel as being one and the same. Dwight Pentecost has listed no fewer than twenty-four (24) clear distinctions between Israel and the Church. These two groups cannot be united as one." [63]

The Ministry of the 144,000

We believe the 144,000 Jews who are sealed will perform a very important ministry during the Tribulation. They are part of God's answer to the question: *How can anyone be saved during the Tribulation with the church gone?"*

How will they hear the Gospel? There will be three channels God will use during the Tribulation to get the Gospel to those who have never heard.

- The 144,000 Jews (7:1-8) (14:1-5) will preach.

- The two witnesses (Rev. 11:3-12) will preach.

- The Angel with the Everlasting Gospel (Rev. 14:6) will preach.

---

[63]Dwight Pentecost, Outlines of Things to Come (Grand Rapids: Zondervan, 1958) pages 201-202.

- The sealing of the 144,000 will be a fulfillment of Matthew 24:14, where Jesus said: *"And this gospel of the kingdom shall be preached in all the world for a witness unto all nations; and then shall the end come."*

John Walvoord: "The prevalent idea that the church is the true Israel is not sustained by any explicit reference in the Bible, and the word 'Israel' is never used of Gentiles, and refers only to those who are racially descendants of Israel or Jacob."[64]

Ray Summers: "A distinction between Jew and Gentile Christians is not drawn elsewhere in the Revelation." [65]

Post-Millennialist: "The literal interpretation is held not only by Premillennarians, but by Post-Millennarians such as Charles Hodge and A-millennarians such as Hendrickson."[66]

Reform Theology: Loraine Boettner wrote: *"Another of the strange doctrines of dispensationalism is that, despite the fact that the Holy Spirit is absent during the Tribulation, a Jewish remnant turns to God and is sealed, and then goes through the world preaching the Gospel. . ."*[67]

The Great Multitude (Rev. 7:9-17)

This part of the vision indicates that a great number of non-Jews will be saved during the Tribulation. There will be converts from every nation, tribe, and language under heaven. The language of the text is very explicit.

---

[64]Walvoord, page 142
[65]Sumnmers, page 148
[66]Walvoord, page 143
[67]Loraine Boettner, The Millennium (Philadelphia: Presbyterian and reformed Publishing Company, 1957) pages 185, 187.

The 144,000 are Jews and the unnumbered multitude are Gentiles.

Where did these people come from? There is no question as to where this group comes from. They came out of the Great Tribulation. There is no room for silly speculation here. Read verse 14 again

Martyrs: Evidently the 144,000 were sealed so they could not be killed as they carried out their Divine mission. In contrast to this, this large group of Gentiles evidently lost their lives for their faith, or died in one of the plagues. For example, they will no longer hunger, thirst, or be tormented by the heat. These are clear references to the judgments that will come during the Tribulation.

OTHER INTERPRETATIONS

Premillennial: John Walvoord[68] would agree with this present writer.

Amillennial: Summers wrote: "The two visions must represent the same group under different circumstances. In one they are sealed and safe as judgment rains down on the earth. . . In the second division, they are seen after they have come through the difficulties."[69]

Reform Theology: Loraine Boettner, referring to Matthew 24:24, said: "Hence Christ referred not to a preaching of the Gospel in our day, or near the end of the age, but to a preaching that was to come before the destruction of Jerusalem in the year A.D. 70."[70] Likewise, the end referred to by Matthew refers not to the end of the world,

---

[68]Walvoord, pages 144-146
[69]Summers, page 152-153
[70]Boettner, page 192

but the end of the Old Testament economy, with the temple, the priesthood, its ritual, its sacrifices, and the final breakup of the Jewish nation."

SUMMARY

What Gospel? What did Jesus say will be preached unto all nations? He said, the "Gospel of the Kingdom."

The first sermon John the Baptist preached was about the Kingdom.

The first sermon Jesus preached was about the Kingdom.

The last question the disciples asked Jesus was "Will you at this time restore the Kingdom to Israel?"[71]

We don't preach the Gospel of the Kingdom. We preach the *Gospel of Grace.*

After the church departs the earth at the Rapture, God will use these 144,000 witness to go into all the world and to preach the Gospel of the Kingdom. The entire Tribulation will last just seven years, and if those 144,000 Jews preached about the coming Kingdom at the very beginning of that period, the Kingdom could be no further than 61,320 hours away.[72]

---

[71] Acts 1:6-7
[72] Multiply 7 years x 365 days x 24 hours

CHAPTER 8

THE TRUMPET JUDGMENTS

Revelation 8:1-4

This chapter describes in detail, some of the judgments that will fall upon the earth during that dreadful period called The Tribulation.

In our opinion, the church is called up to heaven in Revelation 4:1 and the events between chapters 4 and 19 take place after the church has been removed from earth and taken by Christ to a place of safety.

The terrible judgments that are about to fall on the earth will not fall on the church.

Silence in Heaven

"And when he had opened the seventh seal, there was silence in heaven about the space of half an hour. This silence reminds us of the silence in a court of law when the jury returns from deliberation and their decision is about to be delivered. The courtroom is silent and every eye is on the Foreman of the Jury. The Foreman is about to read the decision of the jury and the judge will soon pronounce his sentence upon the defendant. In this scene, God is about to pronounce His just decision on a Sin-loving, God-hating, Christ-rejecting earth.

Seven Angels

²And I saw the seven angels which stood before God; and to them were given seven trumpets.

Another Angel

"And another angel came and stood at the altar, having a golden censer; and there was given unto him much incense, that he should offer it with the prayers of all saints upon the golden altar which was before the throne. This Angel is probably Jesus Christ Himself. Jesus appeared many times in the Old Testament as "**The Angel** of the Lord."

(1 Timothy 2:5-6): *"For there is one God, and one mediator between God and men, the man Christ Jesus; Who gave himself a ransom for all, to be testified in due time."*

(Hebrews 7:24-25): *"But this man, because he continueth ever, hath an unchangeable priesthood. Wherefore he is able also to save them to the uttermost that come unto God by him, seeing he ever liveth to make intercession for them."*

The Prayers of the Saints:

⁴And the smoke of the incense, which came with the prayers of the saints, ascended up before God out of the angel's hand. These prayers are perhaps the prayers of the martyred saints in chapter 6 who ask God how long it will be before He judges the wicked men on earth who are killing God's servants.

Incense

Incense was used when the priests went into the House of

God to pray for the people. The incense was made of a special formula and it was so holy common people were forbidden to make it.[73] It was a sweet-smelling smoke that ascended up before God.

Prayer Pleases God

The sweet-smelling incense suggests that God is pleased when His people come to Him in prayer. Another verse that reveals how pleased God is when His children think of Him and talk about Him is found in Malachai 3:16-18.

"Then they that feared the LORD spake often one to another: and the LORD hearkened, and heard it, and a book of remembrance was written before him for them that feared the LORD, and that thought upon his name.

And they shall be mine, saith the LORD of hosts, in that day when I make up my jewels; and I will spare them, as a man spareth his own son that serveth him. Then shall ye return, and discern between the righteous and the wicked, between him that serveth God and him that serveth him not."

Censer of Fire

[5]*And the angel took the censer, and filled it with fire of the altar, and cast it into the earth: and there were voices, and thunderings, and lightnings, and an earthquake.* [6]*And the seven angels which had the seven trumpets prepared themselves to sound."*

---

[73]Exodus 30:34-38

Seven Trumpets

Trumpets were used for many occasions in the Old Testament. [74] John Walvoord reminds us that trumpets were used to: Give the Law; call a public assembly; to direct soldiers; to signal important events; to announce the first of the month, and to announce almost every important occasion.[75]

1. The First Angel

[7]The first angel sounded, and there followed hail and fire mingled with blood, and they were cast upon the earth: and the third part of trees was burnt up, and all green grass was burnt up."

Scorched Earth

This judgment is directed at the earth's vegetation. In this one plague alone, one-third of all the trees on earth are destroyed and all of the green grass is burned up. This is an ecological nightmare. The damage is done by a combination of hail, fire, and blood.

This has happened before, but not to such a great extent. When God sent hail on the land of Egypt,[76] there was fire mingled with the hail. Some of the Egyptians feared God and believed Moses.

They sought shelter for themselves and their animals and survived. Those who ignored Moses' warnings and remained outside lost their lives and that of their livestock.

---

[74] Numbers 10:1-10 & Ezekiel 33:1-7.
[75] Walvoord, page 152
[76] See Exodus 9:18-26

(Exodus 9:23-26) *"And Moses stretched forth his rod toward heaven: and the LORD sent thunder and hail, and the fire ran along upon the ground; and the LORD rained hail upon the land of Egypt.*

²⁴So there was hail, and fire mingled with the hail, very grievous, such as there was none like it in all the land of Egypt since it became a nation.

²⁵And the hail smote throughout all the land of Egypt all that was in the field, both man and beast; and the hail smote every herb of the field, and broke every tree of the field.

²⁶Only in the land of Goshen, where the children of Israel were, was there no hail."

2. The second angel (Rev. 8:8-9)

⁸"And the second angel sounded, and as it were a great mountain burning with fire was cast into the sea: and the third part of the sea became blood;

⁹And the third part of the creatures which were in the sea, and had life, died; and the third part of the ships were destroyed."

In this judgment, a giant meteor falls into the oceans and kills one-third of all of the sea-life and one-third of all the ships as well. While doing research on meteorites, this present writer came across two things you may find interesting.

Dinosaurs became extinct: The first article was written by a scientist who believes that dinosaurs became extinct because a meteor fell on the earth years ago. He even has a map showing where he believes the meteor fell near the Yucatan   Peninsula. (www.etsu.edu/physics/plntrm/dino/end.htm)

139

Doomsday asteroid: During the same research, we came across evidence in which scientist say that a giant asteroid is heading to the earth and will hit the earth on February 1, 2019 AD.

24 JULY 2002 BBC NEWS

Scientists are tracking a newly discovered Asteroid, 2002 NT7. "Preliminary reports show this Asteroid, which is about two miles in circumference, is on a Collision Course with earth and early projections show Impact on 1 FEB 2019 AD. In the worst case scenario, a disaster of this size would be global in its extent, would create a meltdown of our economic and social life, and would reduce us to dark age conditions. If it did hit the Earth it would cause a continental-size explosion, " said Dr. Benny Peiser, an asteroid expert at Liverpool John Moore's University in northern England.

3. The Third Angel (Rev. 8)

[10]And the third angel sounded, and there fell a great star from heaven, burning as it were a lamp, and it fell upon the third part of the rivers, and upon the fountains of waters;

[11]And the name of the star is called Wormwood: and the third part of the waters became wormwood; and many men died of the waters, because they were made bitter."

In this judgment, a burning stars falls onto the earth and poisons the water supply. Again, this is similar to the plagues God sent on Egypt by the hand of Moses and Aaron (Exodus 7:19-21).

And the LORD spake unto Moses, Say unto Aaron, Take thy rod, and stretch out thine hand upon the waters of Egypt, upon their streams, upon their rivers, and upon their ponds, and upon all their pools of water, that they may become blood; and that there may be blood throughout all the land of Egypt, both in vessels of wood, and in vessels of stone.

20And Moses and Aaron did so, as the LORD commanded; and he lifted up the rod, and smote the waters that were in the river, in the sight of Pharaoh, and in the sight of his servants; and all the waters that were in the river were turned to blood.

21And the fish that was in the river died; and the river stank, and the Egyptians could not drink of the water of the river; and there was blood throughout all the land of Egypt."

4. The Fourth Angel (Rev. 8)

12And the fourth angel sounded, and the third part of the sun was smitten, and the third part of the moon, and the third part of the stars; so as the third part of them was darkened, and the day shone not for a third part of it, and the night likewise."

Powers of Heaven Shaken: Jesus warned us about this in Luke 21:25-26). We also read about this in Revelation 6:12-13. *"And there shall be signs in the sun, and in the moon, and in the stars; and upon the earth distress of nations, with perplexity; the sea and the waves roaring; Men's hearts failing them for fear, and for looking after those things which are coming on the earth:* ***for the powers of heaven shall be shaken."***

Have you noticed at this point, that God is removing the things (grass, sunshine, rain, fresh water, etc.) He has put here for man's benefit.

God gives these things to the wicked as well as the righteous, but wicked men are never thankful, nor will they give God the glory for creating these things.

Lost men and women just take these things fo granted. Some even worship them (sun, moon, animals, etc.) rather than the God who created them.

Isn't it strange that it's even against the law to teach Intelligent Design in government schools?

(Romans 1:19-25) *"Because that which may be known of God is manifest in them; for God hath showed it unto them.*

20For the invisible things of him from the creation of the world are clearly seen, being understood by the things that are made, even his eternal power and Godhead; so that they are without excuse:

21Because that, when they knew God, they glorified him not as God, neither were thankful; but became vain in their imaginations, and their foolish heart was darkened.

22Professing themselves to be wise, they became fools,

23And changed the glory of the un corruptible God into an image made like to corruptible man, and to birds, and four footed beasts, and creeping things.

25Who changed the truth of God into a lie, and worshiped and served the creature more than the Creator, who is blessed forever. Amen."

Host of Heaven

When God placed man on the earth, He gave him the sun, moon, and the stars so that he could measure time and enjoy the seasons (Genesis 1:14). *"And God said, Let there be lights in the firmament of the heaven to divide the day from the night; and let them be for signs, and for seasons, and for days, and years."*

Men's hearts are so wicked and depraved, they not only fail to thank God for these things, they even deny that God

142

created them.   To make matters worse, they became so perverted they began to worship these things instead of worshiping the God who made them.   In these judgments, God will begin removing those things that men have taken for granted. And the worst is yet to come.

The worst is yet to come (Rev. 8:13) *And I beheld, and heard an angel flying through the midst of heaven, saying with a loud voice, Woe, woe, woe, to the inhabiters of the earth by reason of the other voices of the trumpet of the three angels, which are yet to sound!*

CHAPTER 9

THE FIRST AND SECOND WOES

The Falling Star (9:1-2)

[1]"*And the fifth angel sounded, and I saw a star fall from heaven unto the earth: and to him was given the key of the bottomless pit.* [2]*And he opened the bottomless pit; and there arose a smoke out of the pit, as the smoke of a great furnace; and the sun and the air were darkened by reason of the smoke of the pit.*"

Fall or Fallen

Scholars remind us that the word "fall" is in the *perfect tense* which means that it is a *completed action*. There are three different references to falling stars in The Revelation. In chapter six, the stars fall like figs; In chapter 8, a burning meteors fall into the ocean and onto the earth; *Here, we see a different kind of "star."*

A Person

This star is not a meteor, it is a person. Why do we believe this is a person? Look again at verse one. It says "*to him*" was given the key to the bottomless pit. "Him" is a person! We believe the "him" in this verse is Satan.

Bottomless Pit

In these verses, we see Satan, who has fallen from heaven, given the key to the pit (abyss) where fallen angels have been imprisoned since early history. There are other references to Satan falling from (or being cast out of) heaven.

(Isaiah 14:12-17): *12How art thou fallen from heaven, O Lucifer, son of the morning! how art thou cut down to the ground, which didst weaken the nations!*

13For thou hast said in thine heart, I will ascend into heaven, I will exalt my throne above the stars of God: I will sit also upon the mount of the congregation, in the sides of the north:

14I will ascend above the heights of the clouds; I will be like the most High.

15Yet thou shalt be brought down to hell, to the sides of the pit.

16They that see thee shall narrowly look upon thee, and consider thee, saying, Is this the man that made the earth to tremble, that did shake kingdoms;

17That made the world as a wilderness, and destroyed the cities thereof; that opened not the house of his prisoners?

(Luke 10:18): *"And he said unto them, I beheld Satan as lightning fall from heaven."*

The Abyss

This "star" (Satan) is given the key to the abyss (pit) where fallen angels have been imprisoned for centuries.

(2 Peter 2:4): *"For if God spared not the angels that sinned, but cast them down to hell, and delivered them into chains of* *darkness, to be reserved unto judgment."*

(Luke 8:30-31): *"And Jesus asked him, saying, What is thy name? And he said, Legion: because many devils were entered into him. *31*And they besought him that he would not command them to go out into the deep."* **This "pit" is where Satan will be bound for 1000 years during the Millennium.**

(Rev. 20:1-3): *"And I saw an angel come down from heaven, having the key of the bottomless pit and a great chain in his hand.*

2And he laid hold on the dragon, that old serpent, which is the Devil, and Satan, and bound him a thousand years,

3And cast him into the bottomless pit, and shut him up, and set a seal upon him, that he should deceive the nations no more, till the thousand years should be fulfilled: and after that he must be loosed a little season."

There are some who believe that Romans 10:7 implies that Jesus Christ Himself descended into this spirit world in the interval between His death and Resurrection. **(Romans 10:7)** *"Or, Who shall descend into the deep?* (that is, to bring up Christ again from the dead.)

Satan Given the Keys

Jesus holds the keys to death and hades (Rev. 1:18), but for a brief period during the Tribulation, Jesus will give Satan the keys and he will open the pit and release the demons (fallen angels) who are imprisoned there.

(Rev. 9:3-6): *"And there came out of the smoke locusts upon the earth: and unto them was given power, as the scorpions of the earth have power.*

4And it was commanded them that they should not hurt the

147

grass of the earth, neither any green thing, neither any tree; but only those men which have not the seal of God in their foreheads.

⁵And to them it was given that they should not kill them, but that   they should be tormented five months: and their torment was as the torment   of   a scorpion, when he striketh a man. ⁶And in those days shall men seek death, and shall not find it; and shall desire to die, and death shall flee from them."

Who are these demons?

There's a lot of confusion on the subject of demons. There are at least three popular views on this subject.

1. The heathen Greek view is that demons are the **souls of evil people** who have died.

2. Others believe that demons are the **disembodied spirits of a race** of people who lived on earth before God created Adam and Eve.

3. There are others who believe that demons are **the offspring of angels and women** who lived before the flood (See Genesis 6:1-4). These are all false views.

Demons are Fallen Angels

1. Satan Himself is an angel. He is called the "prince of demons" in (Matt. 12:24).

2. Satan has well-organized ranks of angels (Ephesians 6:11-12).

3. Some of these fallen angels (demons) are already confined in the abyss (2 Peter 2:4) (Jude 6).

4. It is reasonable to believe that the demons who are confined are the ones who participated in the sin of (Genesis 6:1-4).

In the opinion of this present writer, these are the sinful, fallen angels who will be released for a season during the Tribulation. Eventually all demons will be cast with Satan into the lake of fire (Matt. 25:41).

Demons Looked like Locusts (9:3-6)

"And there came out of the smoke locusts upon the earth: and unto them was given power, as the scorpions of the earth have power.

⁴And it was commanded them that they should not hurt the grass of the earth, neither any green thing, neither any tree; but only those men which have not the seal of God in their foreheads.

⁵And to them it was given that they should not kill them, but that they should be tormented five months: and their torment was as the torment of a scorpion, when he striketh a man."

⁶And in those days shall men seek death, and shall not find it; and shall desire to die, and death shall flee from them."

Frequently in the Bible, God used locusts to bring judgment upon the earth.[77] In this case, these are not insects – they are men who swarm like insects. People feared a swarm of locusts. When the locusts swarmed over a land they stripped every bush and tree. There was nothing left. In this case, these are demons who swarm like locusts. Their devastation will be unbelievable.

---

[77] Exodus 12:12-20. Joel 1:4-7

Don't Hurt Vegetation

You will notice that God is still in control. He will allow the demons escape from their prison in the abyss, but God still has total control over what they do. God will not allow them to hurt the vegetation or touch the 144,000 who have been "sealed." Their purpose at this point is to torment the wicked, God-hating, Christ-rejecting, sin-loving people who are left on the earth.

Men Will Beg To Die

These demons will cause so much pain that people will beg to die but won't be able. They will try to commit suicide, but they will fail. They will be forced to live and suffer for five long months. Walvoord reminds us that, for the first time in history, all who do not know the Lord Jesus Christ as their Savior will come under demonic possession and affliction.[78]

Four Angels Released at the Euphrates (9:13-15)

"And the sixth angel sounded, and I heard a voice from the four horns of the golden altar which is before God,

[14]Saying to the sixth angel which had the trumpet, Loose the four angels which are bound in the great river Euphrates.

[15]And the four angels were loosed, which were prepared for an hour, and a day, and a month, and a year, for to slay the third part of men."

---

[78]John Walvoord, The Revelation o Jesus Christ (Chicago: Moody Press, 1966) page 164.

Evil Angels

These are not holy angels. Holy angels are not bound. These have been bound and will be released by God for a specific purpose. These evil beings have been kept incarcerated to be released on an exact hour, day, month, and year. They have an evil mission to fulfill. These evil angels will kill another one-third of the earth's population.

If someone is tempted to think that God is being too hard on these people, just remember, this is exactly what the world has always wanted. Lost people want God to leave them alone. They don't want God and/or Christians telling them how to live, what to do, or what not do.

During this period, people will see what it is like to live in a world without a God of love watching over them, trying to save them, and trying to spare them the pain and suffering that sin inevitably brings.

Earlier in the Fourth Seal, one-fourth of the earth's population is killed. Here, an additional one-third is killed. These two judgments alone account for the deaths of one-half of the earth's population at that time.

The Army of 200 Million (9:16-19)

"And the number of the army of the horsemen were two hundred thousand thousand: and I heard the number of them.

17And thus I saw the horses in the vision, and them that sat on them, having breastplates of fire, and of jacinth, and brimstone: and the heads of the horses were as the heads of lions; and out of their mouths issued fire and smoke and brimstone.

18By these three was the third part of men killed, by the fire, and by the smoke, and by the brimstone, which issued out of their mouths.

151

19For their power is in their mouth, and in their tails: for their tails were like unto serpents, and had heads, and with them they do hurt."

The world's largest army

This is the largest army ever assembled in history. For years, numbers like this were believed to be impossible. In our opinion, this is a literal number of literal people.

What nation today could possibly field an army of this size? Could this be an invasion from the orient (China perhaps?).

Men still refuse to Repent (20-21)

"And the rest of the men which were not killed by these plagues yet repented not of the works of their hands, that they should not worship devils, and idols of gold, and silver, and brass, and stone, and of wood: which neither can see, nor hear, nor walk:

21Neither repented they of their murders, nor of their sorceries, nor of their fornication, nor of their thefts."

CHAPTER 10

EATING THE LITTLE BOOK

We believe the events in Chapters 10 and 11 take place during the Great Tribulation. In our opinion, Christ comes for His church in Rev 4:1 when the door is opened in heaven and the voice tells John to "come up hither."

The voice then tells John that he would be shown things which would take place "hereafter." Those things which will take place "hereafter" are things that will take place during the Tribulation period after the church has been "caught up" to heaven.

Chapters 4-19 describe those events which will take place during the Tribulation. That's one reason the word church, which is mentioned over and over in chapters 2-3 is not mentioned again. The church is gone.

Chapter six provides an overview of the entire Tribulation period beginning with the appearance of the man on the white horse (false Christ) and ending with the stars falling from heaven and men hiding in caves and crying for the rocks to cover them as they try to hide from God in His Day of Wrath. The events are studying in these chapters corresponds perfectly with what Jesus taught in Matthew

24:6-19 and 21-22.

(Revelation 10): *"And I saw another mighty angel come down from heaven, clothed with a cloud: and a rainbow was upon his head, and his face was as it were the sun, and his feet as pillars of fire:*

The Angel

Who is this angel? Some say the angel is Christ Himself. This angel is more likely to be a literal mighty angel like Michael who is named in chapter 12.

The little Book

This little book is not the scroll that is opened in Chapter Six. What is in this little book? We don't know because the contents are not revealed.

2And he had in his hand a little book open: and he set his right foot upon the sea, and his left foot on the earth,

3And cried with a loud voice, as when a lion roareth: and when he had cried, seven thunders uttered their voices.

4And when the seven thunders had uttered their voices, I was about to write: and I heard a voice from heaven saying unto me, Seal up those things which the seven thunders uttered, and write them not.

Time has run out

5And the angel which I saw stand upon the sea and upon the earth lifted up his hand to heaven,

6And sware by him that liveth for ever and ever, who created heaven, and the things that therein are, and the earth, and the things that therein are, and the sea, and the things which are therein, that there should be time no longer:

The Mystery

What is this mystery? This is not a revelation of everything man has ever wondered about. This is the completion of the *Mystery of the Kingdom*[79] which had been revealed to the prophets and preached all through the Old Testament.

7 *"But in the days of the voice of the seventh angel, when he shall begin to sound, the mystery of God should be finished, as he hath declared to his servants the prophets."*

8And the voice which I heard from heaven spake unto me again, and said, Go and take the little book which is open in the hand of the angel which standeth upon the sea and upon the earth.

9And I went unto the angel, and said unto him, Give me the little book. And he said unto me, Take it, and eat it up; and it shall make thy belly bitter, but it shall be in thy mouth sweet as honey.

10And I took the little book out of the angel's hand, and ate it up; and it was in my mouth sweet as honey: and as soon as I had eaten it, my belly was bitter.

11And he said unto me, Thou must prophesy again before many peoples, and nations, and tongues, and kings.

Eating the Book

John Walvoord reminds us that "the incident of John eating the book should be compared to the similar experiences of Ezekiel (Ezekiel 2:9-10; 3:1-4; 14) and Jeremiah (Jeremiah 15:16-18)."[80]

---

[79]Secure a copy of The Coming Kingdom, by Pastor Gene Keith.
[80]Walvoord, page 173

155

CHAPTER 11

THE TWO WITNESSES

According to some scholars, this chapter is supposed to be the most difficult to interpret. It is not difficult at all if we stick to the literal interpretation.

- The City is literal.

- The temple is literal.

- The time periods are literal.

- The two witnesses are literal.

- The earthquake is literal.

- The 7000 people are literally killed.

The Measuring Rod

"And there was given me a reed like unto a rod: and the angel stood, saying, Rise, and measure the temple of God, and the altar, and them that worship therein.

The "reed like a rod" is a tool used for measuring, like a tape measure or a surveyor's tool. The act of measuring the temple seems to signify ownership. It is as God is surveying His property. This could also suggest that the worshipers do not measure up to God's standards. There have been other situations where temples have been measured.

- In Zechariah 2 a man is seen measuring the temple for judgment.

- Another incident is found in Ezekiel 40 where the temple in the future kingdom is measured.

- Still another reference to measuring is found in Revelation 21 where the New Jerusalem is measured.

Given to the Gentiles

2But the court which is without the temple leave out, and measure it not; for it is given unto the Gentiles: and the holy city shall they tread under foot forty and two months.

The Times of the Gentiles

This reminds us of something Jesus said about the city of Jerusalem and the "Times of the Gentiles." **(Luke 21:24):** *"And Jerusalem shall be trodden down of the Gentiles, until the times of the Gentiles be fulfilled."*

The Jews will build a new temple in Jerusalem during the Tribulation period, after the church has been "caught up." The Jews will have renewed their ancient system of sacrifices and all will go well for a brief period.

You will remember that the temple was always "off limits" to gentiles, and the Holy of Holies was "off limits" everybody but the High Priest, who as allowed to enter on special occasions.

There will be peace during the first half of the Tribulation, but in middle of the Tribulation, the Holy of Holies will be desecrated and become the home of an idol placed there by the world ruler. *This is the abomination of d*esolation spoken of by Daniel the Prophet.

Paul's Outline OF These Events

Paul gives us an outline of this in second chapter of Second Thessalonians.

(2 Thess. 2:3-5): *"Let no man deceive you by any means: for that day shall not come, except there come a falling away first, and that man of sin be revealed, the son of perdition;*

4Who opposeth and exalteth himself above all that is called God, or that is worshipped; so that he as God sitteth in the temple of God, showing himself that he is God.

5Remember ye not, that, when I was yet with you, I told you these things?

(Rev. 13:13-18): *"And he doeth great wonders, so that he maketh fire come down from heaven on the earth in the sight of men,*

14And deceiveth them that dwell on the earth by the means of those miracles which he had power to do in the sight of the beast; saying to them that dwell on the earth, that they should make an image to the beast, which had the wound by a sword, and did live.

15And he had power to give life unto the image of the beast, that the image of the beast should both speak, and cause that as many as would not worship the image of the beast should be killed.

16And he causeth all, both small and great, rich and poor, free and bond, to receive a mark in their right hand, or in their foreheads:

¹⁷And that no man might buy or sell, save he that had the mark, or the name of the beast, or the number of his name.
¹⁸Here is wisdom. Let him that hath understanding count the number of the beast: for it is the number of a man; and his number is Six hundred threescore and six."

(Daniel 9:27): *"And he shall confirm the covenant with many for one week: and in the midst of the week he shall cause the sacrifice and the oblation to cease, and for the overspreading of abominations he shall make it desolate, even until the consummation, and that determined shall be poured upon the desolate."*

(Daniel 12:11): *"And from the time that the daily sacrifice shall be taken away, and the abomination that maketh desolate set up, there shall be a thousand two hundred and ninety days."*

(Matt. 24:15-22): *"When ye therefore shall see the abomination of desolation, spoken of by Daniel the prophet, stand in the holy place, (whoso readeth, let him understand)*

¹⁶*Then let them which be in Judaea flee into the mountains:*

¹⁷*Let him which is on the housetop not come down to take any thing out of his house:*

¹⁸*Neither let him which is in the field return back to take his clothes.*

¹⁹*And woe unto them that are with child, and to them that give suck in those days!*

²⁰*But pray ye that your flight be not in the winter, neither on the sabbath day:*

²¹*For then shall be great tribulation, such as was not since the*

beginning of the world to this time, no, nor ever shall be.

22And except those days should be shortened, there should no flesh be saved: but for the elect's sake those days shall be shortened.

The two witnesses (Rev. 11)

3And I will give power unto my two witnesses, and they shall prophesy a thousand two hundred and threescore days, clothed in sackcloth.

4These are the two olive trees, and the two candlesticks standing before the God of the earth.

5And if any man will hurt them, fire proceedeth out of their mouth, and devoureth their enemies: and if any man will hurt them, he must in this manner be killed.

WHO ARE THESE TWO WITNESSES?

Who are these two individuals? There are many different opinions but we cannot be dogmatic about it.

1. Some believe they represent Israel and the church.

2. Others believe they are Enoch and Elijah. Enoch and Elijah are the only two men in the Bible who have never died. Both of those men were "raptured," which means "caught up."

3. Still others say they are Moses and Elijah because of the similarity of the plagues and power displayed.

4. There is evidence to support the idea that Moses and Elijah could be the witnesses.

5. The prophet Malachi (Mal. 4:5) predicted that Elijah would return before the dreadful Day of the Lord.

6. We believe John the Baptist was a partial fulfillment of this prophecy (See Matt. 17:10-13) (Mark 9:11-13) and (Luke 1:17).

7. Additional support for Moses and Elijah is the fact that they both appeared on the Mount of Transfiguration and were seen by Peter, James, and John (Matt. 17:3).

8. Some believe these two witnesses will be two individuals who are saved during the Great Tribulation.

We cannot be dogmatic about this because we really don't know who these two men are. What we do know is that two literal, human witnesses will appear for a brief period and Divine power and protection. They will have the power to stop the rain, turn water into blood, and bring down fire from heaven.

[6]These have power to shut heaven, that it rain not in the days of their prophecy: and have power over waters to turn them to blood, and to smite the earth with all plagues, as often as they will.

Two witnesses killed

"And when they shall have finished their testimony, the beast that ascendeth out of the bottomless pit shall make war against them, and shall overcome them, and kill them.

The unholy Trinity

This is the first of thirty-six (36) references in The Revelation to "The Beast."

1. The Beast out of the pit is Satan himself.

2. The *Beast out of the sea* is the world dictator (Rev. 13:1).

3. The *Beast out of the earth* is the False Religious Leader of that day (Rev. 13:11).

Killed in Jerusalem (Rev. 11)

8And their dead bodies shall lie in the street of the great city, which spiritually is called odom and Egypt, where also our Lord was crucified.

9And they of the people and kindreds and tongues and nations shall see their dead bodies three days and an half, and shall not suffer their dead bodies to be put in graves.

10And they that dwell upon the earth shall rejoice over them, and make merry, and shall send gifts one to another; because these two prophets tormented them that dwelt on the earth.

Worldwide celebration

The deaths of the two witnesses will be an occasion for a world-wide celebration of the enemies of Christ. We can just imagine TV crews from ABC, NBC, & CNN on the scene in Jerusalem sending pictures by satellite into living rooms all over the world.

Resurrected & caught up

But the partying only lasts for three and one-half days. Then, suddenly, while the whole world is watching on television, an amazing thing happens.

11And after three days and an half the Spirit of life from God entered into them, and they stood upon their feet; and great fear fell upon them which saw them.

12And they heard a great voice from heaven saying unto them,

Come up hither. And they ascended up to heaven in a cloud; and their enemies beheld them.

Great earthquake

13*And the same hour was there a great earthquake, and the tenth part of the city fell, and in the earthquake were slain of men seven thousand: and the remnant were affrighted, and gave glory to the God of heaven.*

14*The second woe is past; and, behold, the third woe cometh quickly.*

15*And the seventh angel sounded; and there were great voices in heaven, saying, the kingdoms of this world are become the kingdoms of our Lord, and of his Christ; and he shall reign for ever and ever.*

16*And the four and twenty elders, which sat before God on their seats, fell upon their faces, and worshiped God,*

17*Saying, We give thee thanks, O Lord God Almighty, which art, and wast, and art to come; because thou hast taken to thee thy great power, and hast reigned.*

18*And the nations were angry, and thy wrath is come, and the time of the dead, that they should be judged, and that thou shouldest give reward unto thy servants the prophets, and to the saints, and them that fear thy name, small and great; and shouldest destroy them which destroy the earth."*

19*And the temple of God was opened in heaven, and there was seen in his temple the ark of his testament: and there were lightnings, and voices, and thunderings, and an earthquake, and great hail."*

CHAPTER 12

THE WOMAN AND THE CHILD

When we come to chapter twelve we are introduced to seven great actors. They are:

1. The woman (Israel).

2. The Dragon (Satan).

3. The man-child (Christ).

4. Michael (the angel)

5. The Remnant (The remnant of the seed of the woman).

6. The Beast out of the Sea (The world Dictator).

7. The Beast out of the earth (The false world religious leader).

FOUR IMPORTANT WOMEN

1. Jezebel (Rev. 2:20)

2. The Harlot (17:1-7)

3. The Bride - the Lamb's wife (19:7)

4. The Woman mentioned here.

Who is the woman in this chapter?

1"And there appeared a great wonder in heaven; a woman clothed with the sun, and the moon under her feet, and upon her head a crown of twelve stars: 2 And she being with child cried, travailing in birth, and pained to be delivered."

This woman is Israel

Who is this woman? She is not the church. She is Israel. Why do we identify her as Israel?

1. The first reason is, in Joseph's dream in Genesis 37, the sun and the moon represented his parents, Jacob and Rachael. The stars represented Joseph's brothers (Genesis 37:9-11)."*And he dreamed yet another dream, and told it his brethren, and said, Behold, I have dreamed a dream more; and, behold, **the sun and the moon** and the eleven stars made obeisance to me. And he told it to his father, and to his brethren: and his father rebuked him, and said unto him, What is this* *dream that thou hast dreamed?* **Shall I and thy mother and thy brethren indeed come to bow down ourselves to thee to the earth?** *And his brethren envied him; but his father observed the saying.*

In the thirteenth chapter of the Revelation, this woman is Israel and the twelve stars are the twelve sons of Jacob (the patriarchs).

2. A second reason we believe this woman is Israel is because in the Old Testament, Israel is often presented as the wife of Jehovah. She is often presented as being unfaithful to her husband. In Revelation 13, we believe the woman represents the godly remnant of Israel who will be standing true to God during the Great Tribulation.[81]

The dragon is Satan

3 *"And there appeared another wonder in heaven; and behold a great red dragon, having seven heads and ten horns, and seven crowns upon his heads."*

Satan is called the Dragon in verses 12:7 & 12:9. The seven heads and ten horns are similar to the creature described by Daniel in (Daniel 7:7-8,24).

One third of the stars

4 *"And his tail drew the third part of the stars of heaven, and did cast them to the earth: and the dragon stood before the woman which was ready to be delivered, for to devour her child as soon as it was born."*

Satan, the Dragon, drew one-third of the stars of heaven with him. There are two different ways to interpret this.

---

[81]John Walvoord, <u>The Revelation of Jesus Christ</u> (Chicago: Moody Press,) p. 188

This could mean that Satan will have a large portion of the earth under his control at this point in the Tribulation.

A more popular interpretation is that when Satan rebelled against God,[82] one-third of the angels (stars) in heaven supported Satan in rebellion against God and as a result, they were cast out with Him.

Angels are created beings and originally, God placed them over certain areas of our universe. These stars (angels) are the "Principalities" mentioned in Ephesians 6.

This dragon was waiting for the birth of the man-child (Christ) and had planned to destroy Him the moment He is born. This literally happened! When Jesus was born, Satan used Herod, an Edomite, to kill all of the male children around Bethlehem who were two years old or younger in an attempt to kill baby Jesus (Matthew 2:16-18).

During Jesus' earthly ministry, people tried to throw Jesus off of a cliff. Satan thought he had won the battle when they nailed Him to the cross. But three days later, Jesus won the victory over Satan by rising from the dead.

Later, Jesus ascended into heaven in full view of more than 500 eye-witnesses, most of whom were still alive when Paul wrote First Corinthians 15.

The man child (Rev. 12:5a)

5 And she brought forth a man child, who was to rule all nations with a rod of iron: and her child was caught up unto God, and to his throne." **The man-child is definitely Jesus.** Jesus will someday rule the nations with a rod of iron.

---

[82] Ezekiel 28:15

(Psalm 2:8-9) *"Ask of me, and I shall give thee the heathen for thine inheritance, and the uttermost parts of the earth for thy possession. ⁹Thou shalt break them with a rod of iron; thou shalt dash them in pieces like a potter's vessel."*

(Rev. 19:15-16) *"And out of his mouth goeth a sharp sword, that with it he should smite the nations: and he shall rule them with a rod of iron: and he treadeth the winepress of the fierceness and wrath of Almighty God. ¹⁶And he hath on his vesture and on his thigh a name written, KING OF KINGS, AND LORD OF LORDS."*

Caught up (Rev. 12:5b)

The man-child was "caught up" to the throne of God. These verses give us a panorama of the birth, life, and ascension of Jesus Christ.

The woman fled (Rev. 12:6)

6"And the woman fled into the wilderness, where she hath a place prepared of God, that they should feed her there a thousand two hundred and threescore days."

Satan has always hated Israel because God chose Israel to bring Christ into the world. Satan's followers hate Israel as well. It has always been that way.

There will be peace for the first half of the Tribulation, when the Anti-Christ makes peace with the Jews. During the last half, great persecution will break out against Israel, and God has prepared a place somewhere in the wilderness to protect this godly remnant of Israel.

Satan cast out of heaven (Rev. 12:7-9)

7"And there was war in heaven: Michael and his angels fought against the dragon; and the dragon fought and his angels,

8 and prevailed not; neither was their place found any more in heaven.

9 And the great dragon was cast out, that old serpent, called the Devil, and Satan, which deceiveth the whole world: he was cast out into the earth, and his angels were cast out with him."

This is a literal war in a literal heaven where a literal Satan is literally cast down to a literal earth. Some have objected to the literal interpretation of this saying that Satan is a "spiritual being." **Literal does not necessarily mean "physical."** *Literal means real.* God is a Spirit and God is real. Satan is an angel and he is real. This is a war, not a battle and it is between two sets of spirit men."[83]

Description of Satan (Rev. 12:9)

The description of Satan in verse 9 is important. He is called "The Great Dragon." This applies to the empire He dominates. Satan has many names and His names describe His work. Charles Ryrie has an interesting chart in his study Bible that gives those names and their meaning.[84]

1. **Satan** means Adversary

2. **Devil** means Slanderer

3. **Old Serpent** refers to the deceiver in the Garden of Eden.

4. **God of this world** means that he controls the philosophy of this present world.

---

[83] Patrick Heron
[84] Page 2029

170

5. Ruler of this world means that he rules the world system.

6. Prince and Power of the Air means he exercises control over all unbelievers.

7. **Great Red Dragon** means that he is a destructive creature (Rev. 12:3,7,9)

Satan is the Accuser (Rev. 12: 10-12)

10 *"And I heard a loud voice saying in heaven, Now is come salvation, and strength, and the kingdom of our God, and the power of his Christ: for the accuser of our brethren is cast down, which accused them before our God day and night.*

[11]*And they overcame him by the blood of the Lamb, and by the word of their testimony; and they loved not their lives unto the death.*

[12]*Therefore rejoice, ye heavens, and ye that dwell in them. Woe to the inhabiters of the earth and of the sea! for the devil is come down unto you, having great wrath, because he knoweth that he hath but a short time."*

Satan opposes Christ and His work in three ways. Christ presented Himself as 1) Prophet, 2) Priest, and 3) King. Satan has come against Christ in all of these offices.

1. As the accuser, Satan opposes Christ as our High Priest. Satan accuses believes day and night.

2. When Satan brings forth the First Beast (to be worshiped), He is opposing Christ as King.

3. When Satan brings on the second Beast (false prophet), he is opposing Christ as Prophet.

Daniel predicted this war in heaven many years ago in (Daniel 12:1). *"And at that time shall Michael stand up, the great prince which standeth for the children of thy people: and there shall be a time of trouble, such as never was since there was a nation even to that same time: and at that time thy people shall be delivered, every one that shall be found written in the book."*

Satan was cast out of heaven years ago when he led a rebellion against God. However, Satan has still had access to heaven where he slanders God's people and accuses them before God just as he accused Job.[85]   At this point in the Tribulation, Satan is cast out forever and no longer has access at all. This is when the Tribulation really heats up for Satan is "ticked."

Victory over Satan (Rev. 12:11)

[11]And they overcame him by the blood of the Lamb, and by the word of their testimony; and they loved not their lives unto the death."

THREE THINGS GAVE THE SAINTS VICTORY OVER SATAN

1. The *Blood of the Lamb* nullified the accusations of Satan when he accused them.

2. **Their Testimony** nullified the deceiving work of Satan.

3. **Their willingness to die for Christ** made them totally victorious.

---

[85]Read the first part of the book of Job to get an idea of how this works.

Flying into the wilderness (Rev. 12:13-16)

13"And when the dragon saw that he was cast unto the earth, he persecuted the woman which brought forth the man child.

14And to the woman were given two wings of a great eagle, that she might fly into the wilderness, into her place, where she is nourished for a time, and times, and half a time, from the face of the serpent.

15And the serpent cast out of his mouth water as a flood after the woman, that he might cause her to be carried away of the flood. 16And the earth helped the woman, and the earth opened her mouth, and swallowed up the flood which the dragon cast out of his mouth."

The Dragon and the Remnant (Rev. 12:17)

17 "And the dragon was wroth with the woman, and went to make war with the remnant of her seed, which keep the commandments of God, and have the testimony of Jesus Christ."

During this time of intense persecution Satan will try his best to destroy this tiny remnant of believing Jews. They will escape miraculously as with wings, to this place of safety. Satan will also try to destroy Israel with a flood, but God will also protect them from the waters.

Patrick Heron reminds us that in chapter 8, John saw what looked like a "burning mountain" fall into the sea. As a result of this, one-third of all of the boats in the sea were destroyed.

Heron continued: "Now, if you saw a volcano, and you did not know what it was, you would describe it as a burning mountain. And scientists tell us that if La Palma, an active volcano in the Canary Islands, falls into the sea, it will cause a tsunami hundreds of feet high. Now, Israel is situated not far from this area in North Africa. And there is

173

a clear run for a Tsunami across the Mediterranean. And Israel is on the coast. Perhaps this is why, in Matthew 24, Jesus warns when you see these things happening, 'Let him that is in Judea flee to the mountains.' Because, if there is a Tsunami coming, you want to get to higher ground."[86]

---

[86] Patrick Heron, raptureready.com

CHAPTER 13

THE BEAST AND THE FALSE PROPHET

In this chapter we come to the most commonly discussed part of The Revelation: The "Beast" and the "Mark of the Beast" and the numbers "666." We've all heard of the Anti-Christ, His mark, and the time that was supposed to come when nobody will be allowed to buy or sell unless they had the "Mark of the Beast" on his/her hand or forehead. Well, this is the chapter where this will be discussed.

(Revelation 13:1-10)

1 Then I stood on the sand of the sea. And I saw a beast rising up out of the sea, having seven heads and ten horns, and on his horns ten crowns, and on his heads a blasphemous name.

2 Now the beast which I saw was like a leopard, his feet were like the feet of a bear, and his mouth like the mouth of a lion. The dragon gave him his power, his throne, and great authority.

3 And I saw one of his heads as if it had been mortally wounded, and his deadly wound was healed. And all the world marveled and followed the beast.

4 So they worshiped the dragon who gave authority to the beast;

and they worshiped the beast, saying, "Who is like the beast? Who is able to make war with him?"

5 And he was given a mouth speaking great things and blasphemies, and he was given authority to continue for forty-two months.

6 Then he opened his mouth in blasphemy against God, to blaspheme His name, His tabernacle, and those who dwell in heaven.

7 It was granted to him to make war with the saints and to overcome them. And authority was given him over every tribe, tongue, and nation.

8 All who dwell on the earth will worship him, whose names have not been written in the Book of Life of the Lamb slain from the foundation of the world.

9 If anyone has an ear, let him hear.

10 He who leads into captivity shall go into captivity; he who kills with the sword must be killed with the sword. Here is the patience and the faith of the saints.

(Revelation 13:11-18)11 Then I saw another beast coming up out of the earth, and he had two horns like a lamb and spoke like a dragon.

12 And he exercises all the authority of the first beast in his presence, and causes the earth and those who dwell in it to worship the first beast, whose deadly wound was healed.

13 He performs great signs, so that he even makes fire come down from heaven on the earth in the sight of men.

14 And he deceives those who dwell on the earth by those signs which he was granted to do in the sight of the beast, telling those

176

who dwell on the earth to make an image to the beast who was wounded by the sword and lived.

15 He was granted power to give breath to the image of the beast, that the image of the beast should both speak and cause as many as would not worship the image of the beast to be killed.

16 He causes all, both small and great, rich and poor, free and slave, to receive a mark on their right hand or on their foreheads,

17 and that no one may buy or sell except one who has the mark or the name of the beast, or the number of his name.

18 Here is wisdom. Let him who has understanding calculate the number of the beast, for it is the number of a man: His number is 666.

There are two beasts

There are two Beasts in this chapter. The first Beast comes out of the sea and the second Beast comes out of the earth. The Beast who comes out of the sea is the Anti-Christ. The Beast that comes out of the earth is the False Prophet.

Who are these beasts?

Down through the centuries people have tried to identify these "beasts." There is no end to the speculation of the identity of these creatures. Some say the Beast is Judas; some say he was Nero; others have said he was Hitler, Stalin, Kennedy, Osama Bin Laden, and George W. Bush.

A World Empire

In the opinion of this present writer, the Beast out of the Sea is an empire that will be ruled by an individual. This individual will rule the whole world during the

Tribulation period.

The False Prophet

The second beast (out of the earth) will be a person we call the "False Prophet." The False Prophet will be a religious leader whom Satan will use during this period to persuade the whole world to worship the Beast who came out of the sea.

An Unholy Trinity

Have you noticed that what we have here is an *unholy trinity*? We have Satan, the Beast, and the False Prophet. This unholy trinity will set itself up to war against the Holy Trinity: God the Father, God the Son, and God the Holy Spirit.

The beast out of the sea

We believe the "sea" that the first beast comes out of represents the people and nations (especially in the area around the Mediterranean Sea). We base this on Rev. 17:15. *"Then he said to me, "The waters which you saw, where the harlot sits, are peoples, multitudes, nations, and tongues."* We believe this will be an empire ruled by an individual. In our opinion, this empire will be composed of the countries that once made up the Roman Empire.

Heads, horns, and crowns

In our opinion, the Seven Heads are seven empires out of the past. The Ten Horns are the rulers (leaders) of the ten nations that make up the revived Roman Empire which will be under the control of the Beast during the Tribulation. Why do we believe this? Go back and read the second chapter of the book of Daniel.

(Daniel 2:44) *"And in the days of these kings the God of heaven will set up a kingdom which shall never be destroyed; and the kingdom shall not be left to other people; it shall break in pieces and consume all these kingdoms, and it shall stand forever."*

(Daniel 7:24) *"The ten horns are ten kings who shall arise from this kingdom. And another shall rise after them; He shall be different from the first ones, And shall subdue three kings."*

(Revelation 17:9-12): *"Here is the mind which has wisdom: The seven heads are seven mountains on which the woman sits.*

There are also seven kings. Five have fallen, one is, and the other has not yet come. And when he comes, he must continue a short time.

And the beast that was, and is not, is himself also the eighth, and is of the seven, and is going to perdition. The ten horns which you saw are ten kings who have received no kingdom as yet, but they receive authority for one hour as kings with the beast."

Notice carefully what is said here

There are seven (7) heads. The **seven** (7) heads were mountains on which the woman sat.

Five (5) of those mountains had already fallen when John wrote The Revelation (Greece, Persia, Babylonia, Assyria, & Egypt).

One (#6) mountain was still standing when John wrote. Another (#7) mountain would come in the future. The Beast (#8) will be come out of the seven that had already fallen.

The Ten (10) horns will be the rulers (leaders) who will rule over the kingdoms under the control of the Beast.

Illustrated by animals

These kingdoms were also illustrated by animals in (Rev. 13:2). *"Now the beast which I saw was like a leopard, his feet were like the feet of a bear, and his mouth like the mouth of a lion. The dragon gave him his power, his throne, and great authority."*

- The leopard represented the Greek Empire under Alexander.
- The Bear represented Persia.
- The Lion represented Babylon.

Deadly wound healed

Down through history, people have tried to identify this with an individual who died a natural death, or was assassinated and miraculously came back to life. Some people were certain this would be Judas Iscariot; others speculated that it would be Lenin, Stalin, Hitler, John F. Kennedy, and recently, Osama Bin Laden.

The beast is an empire

In our honest opinion, this "beast" is an empire - - not an individual. This will be the revived Roman Empire, which for all practical purposes has "died" or has vanished from history. But in the "Last Days," will be revived. That's what is meant by "the deadly wound was healed."

This beast came out of the seven

And the beast that was, and is not, is himself also the eighth, and is of the seven, and is going to perdition" (Rev. 17:11).

This Beast (an empire) that arises out of the sea (#8) must

180

come from one of the seven (7) empires that had already fallen (The Roman Empire of the past). It is difficult, these days, to keep from speculating at this point about the European Union, the United Nations, the Euro-dollar, the World Court, Globalism, etc. We do believe, that in the last days:

1. The Roman Empire will be revived.

2. There will be a one-world government,

3. There will be a one-world (false) religion.

4. And the whole system will be under the control of Satan and the "unholy trinity."

Satan is worshiped

(Rev. 13:4) *So they worshiped the dragon who gave authority to the beast; and they worshiped the beast, saying, "Who is like the beast? Who is able to make war with him?"*

(Rev. 13:8) *"All who dwell on the earth will worship him, whose names have not been written in the Book of Life of the Lamb slain from the foundation of the world."*

Paul predicted this

One of the clearest teachings on this is found in one of Paul's earliest letters to the churches.

(2 Thess. 2:3-12) *3 Let no one deceive you by any means; for that Day will not come unless the falling away comes first, and the man of sin is revealed, the son of perdition,*

4 who opposes and exalts himself above all that is called God or that is worshiped, so that he sits as God, in the temple of God, showing himself that he is God.

5 Do you not remember that when I was still with you I told you these things?

6 And now you know what is restraining, that he may be revealed in his own time.

7 For the mystery of lawlessness is already at work; only He who now restrains will do so until He is taken out of the way.

8 And then the lawless one will be revealed, whom the Lord will consume with the breath of His mouth and destroy with the brightness of His coming.

9 The coming of the lawless one is according to the working of Satan, with all power, signs, and lying wonders,

10 and with all unrighteous deception among those who perish, because they did not receive the love of the truth, that they might be saved.

11 And for this reason God will send them strong delusion, that they should believe the lie,

12 that they all may be condemned who did not believe the truth but had pleasure in unrighteousness.

Satan's Sinful Ambition

Satan has always wanted to be god. He is the "god of this world," but he craves to take the place of God Almighty. This will be his last attempt and it will last but for a short time.

(Isaiah 14:12-17) *12 "How you are fallen from heaven, O Lucifer, son of the morning! How you are cut down to the ground, you who weakened the nations!*

13 For you have said in your heart: 'I will ascend into heaven, I will exalt my throne above the stars of God; I will also sit on the mount of the congregation on the farthest sides of the north;

14 I will ascend above the heights of the clouds, I will be like the Most High.'

15 Yet you shall be brought down to Sheol, To the lowest depths of the Pit.

16 "Those who see you will gaze at you, And consider you, saying: 'Is this the man who made the earth tremble, Who shook kingdoms,

17 Who made the world as a wilderness And destroyed its cities, Who did not open the house of his prisoners?'

He will blaspheme God (13:5-6)

This Evil creature will blaspheme God for 42 months and will gain control over the whole world during this period. During this brief period, the dream of every world dictator will be fulfilled.

Russia and Israel

There's something else that you may find interesting. Jesus said that there would always be "wars and rumors of wars." But in addition to that, the Bible predicts that there will be *three major wars* that will take place in the Latter Days.

One of these major wars will be between Russia and Israel. This war is described in Ezekiel 38-39.

We mentioned this at this point because there is a good possibility that *this battle could take place in our lifetime, before we are "called up"* (Rev. 4:1) **before the Tribulation. begins.**

Muslims in Russian Army

This war is important because Russia will be destroyed in this war. This will remove Russia and most of her allies from the list of "Superpowers," and will make it much easier for this evil world leader to take over the whole world.

There was an article in the Gainesville Sun by Lyric Wallwork Winik, about "coalition forces" in Iraq. **The article was actually in the "Parade" which was included in the Gainesville Sun**. This article provides another reason for Russia to attack Israel in addition to the reasons found in Ezekiel 38.

"Key U.S. policy-makers have largely written off military alliances with Western Europe for efforts in the Middle East and the war on terror. Why? Off the record, they cite Europe's large influx of Islamic immigrants. They believe that many of the leaders in Western Europe are unwilling to antagonize their growing Muslim populations by taking on Islamic radicals or siding with an increasingly unpopular U.S. And it's not just our traditional allies who are being reassessed. Russia is as well.

A quarter of Moscow's 10 million residents are Muslims, and some estimate that the Russian army will be 50% Muslim in less than 10 years.[87]

---

[87]Parade Magazine, Sunday February 25, 2007

CHAPTER 14

THE 144,000 WITNESSES

Marked by God

14 And I looked, and, lo, a Lamb stood on the mount Zion, and with him an hundred forty and four thousand, having his Father's name written in their foreheads.

2 And I heard a voice from heaven, as the voice of many waters, and as the voice of a great thunder: and I heard the voice of harpers harping with their harps:

Sang a new song

3 And they sung as it were a new song before the throne, and before the four beasts, and the elders: and no man could learn that song but the hundred and forty and four thousand, which were redeemed from the earth.

All Jews – all Male – all virgins

4 These are they which were not defiled with women; for they are virgins. These are they which follow the Lamb whithersoever he goeth. These were redeemed from among men, being the first fruits unto God and to the Lamb.

5 *And in their mouth was found no guile: for they are without fault before the throne of God.*

Angel with the everlasting Gospel

6 *And I saw another angel fly in the midst of heaven, having the everlasting gospel to preach unto them that dwell on the earth, and to every nation, and kindred, and tongue, and people,*

7 *Saying with a loud voice, Fear God, and give glory to him; for the hour of his judgment is come: and worship him that made heaven, and earth, and the sea, and the fountains of waters.*

8 *And there followed another angel, saying, Babylon is fallen, is fallen, that great city, because she made all nations drink of the wine of the wrath of her fornication.*

The mark of the Beast

9 *And the third angel followed them, saying with a loud voice, If any man worship the beast and his image, and receive his mark in his forehead, or in his hand,*

10 *The same shall drink of the wine of the wrath of God, which is poured out without mixture into the cup of his indignation; and he shall be tormented with fire and brimstone in the presence of the holy angels, and in the presence of the Lamb:*

11 *And the smoke of their torment ascendeth up for ever and ever: and they have no rest day nor night, who worship the beast and his image, and whosoever receiveth the mark of his name.*

12 *Here is the patience of the saints: here are they that keep the commandments of God, and the faith of Jesus.*

Rest and peace for God's people

13 And I heard a voice from heaven saying unto me, Write, Blessed are the dead which die in the Lord from henceforth: Yea, saith the Spirit, that they may rest from their labors; and their works do follow them.

14 And I looked, and behold a white cloud, and upon the cloud one sat like unto the Son of man, having on his head a golden crown, and in his hand a sharp sickle.

Judgment and death for lost people

15 And another angel came out of the temple, crying with a loud voice to him that sat on the cloud, Thrust in thy sickle, and reap: for the time is come for thee to reap; for the harvest of the earth is ripe.

16 And he that sat on the cloud thrust in his sickle on the earth; and the earth was reaped.

17 And another angel came out of the temple which is in heaven, he also having a sharp sickle.

18 And another angel came out from the altar, which had power over fire; and cried with a loud cry to him that had the sharp sickle, saying, thrust in thy sharp sickle, and gather the clusters of the vine of the earth; for her grapes are fully ripe.

19 And the angel thrust in his sickle into the earth, and gathered the vine of the earth, and cast it into the great winepress of the wrath of God.

20 And the winepress was trodden without the city, and blood came out of the winepress, even unto the horse bridles, by the space of a thousand and six hundred furlongs.

THE SEVEN LAST PLAGUES

From Genesis to The Revelation God has warned men that one day He will judge sin.

In Genesis 6:1, just prior to the flood, God warned, "My Spirit will not always strive with man."

In Numbers 32:23, God warned, "Be sure your sins will find you out."

In Luke 8:17, Jesus warned that one day, all secrets will be brought out into the light.

In Galatians 6:7, we are told plainly that we will all reap what we sow.

In Proverbs 29:1, God warns that those who continually and willfully refuse to listen to the warnings of God will suddenly be destroyed "and that without remedy." Their destruction will be terminal!

Seven last plagues

And I saw another sign in heaven, great and marvellous, seven angels having the seven last plagues; for in them is filled up the wrath of God.

2 And I saw as it were a sea of glass mingled with fire: and them that had gotten the victory over the beast, and over his image, and over his mark, and over the number of his name, stand on the sea of glass, having the harps of God.

3 And they sing the song of Moses the servant of God, and the song of the Lamb, saying, great and marvelous are thy works, Lord God Almighty; just and true are thy ways, thou King of saints.

4 Who shall not fear thee, O Lord, and glorify thy name? for thou only art holy: for all nations shall come and worship before thee; for thy judgments are made manifest.

5 And after that I looked, and, behold, the temple of the tabernacle of the testimony in heaven was opened:

6 And the seven angels came out of the temple, having the seven plagues, clothed in pure and white linen, and having their breasts girded with golden girdles.

7 And one of the four beasts gave unto the seven angels seven golden vials full of the wrath of God, who liveth for ever and ever.

8 And the temple was filled with smoke from the glory of God, and from his power; and no man was able to enter into the temple, till the seven plagues of the seven angels were fulfilled.

The time has come

That time of judgment has finally come for this God-hating, Christ-rejecting, sin-loving world. It is over! Nobody escapes! There's no place to hide! This judgment is terminal!

This judgment is deserved

This judgment is just and right. In fact, this judgment is long overdue. This judgment is exactly what sinful men deserve. If God didn't punish men for their sins then God would be unjust!

How vile lost sinners really are.

Men not only reject God, they reject God's Word, they reject God's Son, they despise God's children (Christians), they despise God's House (the church), and they have no respect for God's Day.

Neither do they appreciate the long time God put off punishing them, giving them time to repent of their sins. We will see in these chapters, how that when their time of judgment finally comes, rather than using their tongues to repent and call on God, they use their tongues to curse God with their dying breath.

God's Wrath (Rev. 15:1)

*"And I saw another sign in heaven, great and marvelous, seven angels having the seven last plagues; for in them is **filled up the wrath of God.**"*

The word *wrath* (Greek *thymos*) means *anger* or *rage*. The expression *filled up* means that it (God's anger) has been brought to a conclusion.

Martyred dead killed by the beast (Rev. 15:2)[1]

[2]And I saw as it were a sea of glass mingled with fire: and them that had gotten the victory over the beast, and over his image, and over his mark, and over the number of his name, stand on the sea of glass, having the harps of God."

Harps and Lyres

Have you noticed that hasps and trumpets are the only instruments mentioned in The Revelation?

Notice also that harps are not given to all martyrs - - just these. No harps were given those in (Rev. 7:9-17).

These harps were given to these martyrs as a reward for refusing to worship the Beast, receiving his mark, or bow before his image. They remained faithful unto death.

They sang two songs (verses 3-4)

[3]And they sing the song of Moses the servant of God, and the song of the Lamb, saying, Great and marvelous are thy works, Lord God Almighty; just and true are thy ways, thou King of saints.

[4]Who shall not fear thee, O Lord, and glorify thy name? for thou only art holy: for all nations shall come and worship before thee; for thy judgments are made manifest."

They sang the *Song of Moses* and the *Song of the Lamb*. **The song of Moses** was a song of God's faithfulness to Israel. **The**

---

[1]We read of this in Rev. 13:1-10

Song of the Lamb was a song of the saints' redemption from sin.

Moses sang one song (Exodus 15) when God parted the Red Sea and the Israelites escaped from Egypt.

Moses sang another song that is recorded in (Deut. 32). This song was personally written by Moses at the close of his career. This song is a comprehensive picture of God's faithfulness and His ultimate purpose to defeat Israel's enemies.

The Tabernacle was opened in Heaven (5-6)

⁵And after that I looked, and, behold, the temple of the tabernacle of the testimony in heaven was opened:

⁶And the seven angels came out of the temple, having the seven plagues, clothed in white linen, and having their breasts girded with golden girdles.
⁷And one of the four beasts gave unto the seven angels seven golden vials full of the wrath of God, who liveth for ever and ever.

⁸And the temple was filled with smoke from the glory of God, and from his power; and no man was able to enter into the temple, till the seven plagues of the seven angels were fulfilled."

CHAPTER 17

IS MYSTERY BABYLON ROME, BABYLON, OR MECCA?

The Scriptures teach that in the final days of history, there will be a "one world" religion, a "one-world government" and a "one-world Ruler (dictator). This world dictator will come to power, partly with the assistance of a false religious system which is described in detail in Revelation, chapter 17. This system is described as a harlot riding on a scarlet colored beast. Who is this woman? What is her name? Where is she located?

THREE THEORIES

1. Mystery Babylon is **Rome and the Vatican.**

2. Mystery Babylon is **literal Babylon.**

3. Mystery **Babylon is Mecca.**

We will present evidence for all three, and as the say on FOX News: "We Report! You Decide!"

(Revelation 17:1-18) *"1 Then one of the seven angels who had the seven bowls came and talked with me, saying to me, 'Come, I will show you the judgment of the **great harlot who sits on***

many waters,

2 with whom the kings of the earth committed fornication, and the inhabitants of the earth were made **drunk with the wine of her fornication.'**

3 So he carried me away in the Spirit into the wilderness. And I saw a woman sitting on a scarlet beast which was full of names of blasphemy, having seven heads and ten horns.

4 The woman was **arrayed in purple and scarlet, and adorned with gold and precious stones and pearls**, *having in her hand a golden cup full of abominations and the filthiness of her fornication.*

5 And on her forehead a name was written: MYSTERY, BABYLON THE GREAT, THE **MOTHER** *OF HARLOTS AND OF THE ABOMINATIONS OF THE EARTH.*

6 I saw the woman, **drunk with the blood of the saints** *and with the blood of the martyrs of Jesus. And when I saw her, I marveled with great amazement.*

7 But the angel said to me, "Why did you marvel? I will tell you the mystery of the woman and of the beast that carries her, which has the seven heads and the ten horns.

8 The beast that you saw was, and is not, and will ascend out of the bottomless pit and go to perdition. And those who dwell on the earth will marvel, whose names are not written in the Book of Life from the foundation of the world, when they see the beast that was, and is not, and yet is."

9 Here is the mind which has wisdom: The seven heads are seven mountains on which the woman sits.

10 There are also seven kings. Five have fallen, one is, and the other has not yet come. And when he comes, he must continue a short time.

11 And the beast that was, and is not, is himself also the eighth, and is of the seven, and is going to perdition.

12 The ten horns which you saw are ten kings who have received no kingdom as yet, but they receive authority for one hour as kings with the beast.

13 These are of one mind, and they will give their power and authority to the beast.

14 These will make war with the Lamb, and the Lamb will overcome them, for He is Lord of lords and King of kings; and those who are with Him are called, chosen, and faithful."

15 Then he said to me, "The waters which you saw, where the harlot sits, are peoples, multitudes, nations, and tongues.

16 And the ten horns which you saw on the beast, these will hate the harlot, make her desolate and naked, eat her flesh and burn her with fire.

17 For God has put it into their hearts to fulfill His purpose, to be of one mind, and to give their kingdom to the beast, until the words of God are fulfilled.

18 And the woman whom you saw is that great city which reigns over the kings of the earth."

WHAT DO WE KNOW ABOUT THIS WOMAN?

A woman

The first clue the writer of The Revelation gives us is that this system is portrayed as a woman riding on the back of an animal (Revelation 17:3).

Her clothing

In (Rev. 17:4), this mysterious woman is pictured as being "arrayed in purple and scarlet color, and bedecked with gold and precious stones and pearls, having a golden cup in her hand, full of abominations and filthiness of her fornication."

Her Name

This woman has two names written on her written on her forehead. One of those names is "Mystery Babylon the Great." She is also called, "The Mother of Harlots, and of the abominations of the earth" (17:5).

Her language

She is said to be full of blasphemy.

She is drunk on blood

This strange looking woman is intoxicated, but not with wine. She is drunk on the blood of God's people (Rev. 17:6). Evidently she is hostile to the true believers who are alive and on the earth at that time.

WHAT DO WE KNOW ABOUT THIS BEAST?

The beast upon which this mysterious woman sits is described in vivid detail in Revelation 17:3.

The Color of the Beast (17:3): The beast upon which this woman is riding, is "scarlet-colored."

Seven Heads: This animal is strange indeed. It has not one, but seven heads.

Ten Horns: This strange animal is also seen as having ten horns.

Religion and Political Power: It is obvious that this woman is not a literal woman, nor is the animal a literal animal.

The woman and the animal *both are symbols* that represent something else. In the opinion of this writer, both the woman and the animal she rides, represent two "systems" that will exist during the end times.

- The woman represents the **religious system** of that period.
- The animal represents the **political system** of that period.
- These two systems (religion & government) will work hand-in-hand for a short time during that period of human history.

Two Separate Powers: The woman is not the animal. She is separate from the animal. The fact that the woman is riding the animal and the animal is carrying her on its back suggests that the two of them are working together.

Using the Beast

The text suggests that the woman is "using" the animal and the animal is "supporting" the woman. Evidently, these two systems, religion and politics, will work "hand-in-hand" to bring the whole world under the control of the coming "one-world government" and the "one-world" dictator.

Hated and destroyed by the Beast

Further evidence that the woman and the animal are two separate systems is the fact that, later in the chapter, we discover that the beast hates the woman, later turns on the woman, and destroys her. The woman (apostate religious system) dies and the animal lives on.

The focus of this chapter is to examine the evidence, *especially the text itself*, and try to accurately identify this mystery woman.

- Who is this woman?
- What religious system does she represent?
- What is her modern name?
- Will her headquarters be Rome, Babylon, or Mecca?

TRADITIONAL VIEW: THE HARLOT IS ROME

With these questions in our minds, let us now consider the traditional interpretation of this important chapter. For as long as this writer can remember, protestant writers and speakers have been unanimous in their belief that this woman is the Catholic Church. This belief has been a part of our tradition for so long, that today, it is accepted without question or reservation.

Peter Ruckman: "There is no doubt about it. The woman is Rome."

Jack Van Impe: Evangelist Jack Van Impe is even more adamant. On page 195 in "Revelation Revealed," the author states emphatically: *"There is absolutely no doubt about it. Romanism is Babylonianism in mystery form."*

Where is the Evidence that supports the traditional view that identifies the Catholic Church as the "Mystery Woman" and the "Great Harlot" of The Revelation?

What is this basis of this interpretation? How can one be *absolutely sure* that Rome is Babylon in mystery form?

Why have Evangelicals and Fundamentalist traditionally identified the Roman Catholic Church with the Great Harlot of Revelation 17?

As far as we can determine, the traditional view, that the woman is the Roman Catholic Church, rests on the following three things:

1. Seven Hills of Rome

The first reason many writers identify the Catholic Church as Mystery Babylon is because of the reference to the *seven mountains in (Rev 17:9)*. *"The seven heads are seven mountains on which the woman sits."* The idea that the city of Rome is the home of the harlot is based on the idea that Rome is commonly known as the City of Seven Hills. This idea is deeply ingrained in protestant tradition.

One writer put it this way: "*Every school boy knows that Rome is the city of seven hills.*" Should we need to be reminded that one does not interpret Scripture based on what some writer assumes every school-boy knows?

Considering the pitiful state of public education today, especially in the area of geography, *it is doubtful that many of today's high-school graduates could even locate the city of Rome on a map of the world,* much less know anything about the topography of that area of Italy.

The argument for the traditional view goes something like this: **Since we already believe** that Rome is Mystery Babylon. **Since everybody knows** that Rome is the *headquarters* of the Catholic Church. . . . **Since everybody knows** that Rome is the city of seven hills, what need is there for further research? The mystery is solved. **Babylon has to be Rome!** *The case is closed! End of conversation.*

2. Protestant Tradition

The second reason many Protestants have accepted the position that the Catholic Church is the Great Whore of Revelation is because of tradition. It is easy for one to understand how that the Reformers[88] and those people living in that period of time, could easily be led to believe that the Catholic Church was Babylon", and that the Pope was the Anti-Christ. This is what all of our popular Evangelist and Pastors have taught us. This is our protestant heritage, so it *must be true.* Since *everybody* says that Rome is Babylon. How can *everybody* be wrong? We've always believed this. We ask you, "Dare we conclude that Rome is Babylon simply because some reformers from another generation, or some popular Evangelists of our day believe this?"

Is it possible that we have become so comfortable with this particular tradition that we have become like the Pharisees of Jesus Day of whom He spoke when He said in (Mark 7:13):*"You have made the Word of God of none effect by your Tradition."* The Pharisees were familiar with the Scriptures. They would be called the *Fundamentalist* of their day. However, they erred by placing their own man-made traditions on the same level as the Word of God.

---

[88]It is only fair to remind our readers that no Reform Theologian's claim to fame has been his contributions in the field of eschatology.

3. Book: The two Babylons

The third, and perhaps the strongest argument for the traditional interpretation of Revelation 17, is the book, *The Two Babylons*, written by Alexander Hislop, and published back in 1916. This book is definitely a classic and Hislops contribution to our understanding of Babylonian religion and its influence upon the Roman Catholic Church must not be under-estimated. However, there are serious problems and weaknesses with the traditional view. The purpose of this study is to take the time to re-examine the evidence and render a "second opinion" on this subject.

THERE ARE PROBLEMS WITH VIEW

If we are to accurately identify Mystery Babylon, we must begin with the Scriptures, not books written about the Scriptures. Before we turn to the commentaries and learn what others have said about this controversial chapter, let's turn again to the Scriptures themselves and see what we can learn.

The Seven Mountains

In (Rev 17:9), the Bible says that beast upon which the woman is riding has seven "horns". The Bible also identifies those "horns" as seven hills or mountains. In the opinion of this writer, it is pre-mature to identify Rome as the home of the harlot based primarily on these references to seven hills or mountains.

If these *seven horns and seven mountains,* we must turn our attention to the city of Rome and ask, "Are there seven hills or mountains inside the city limits of Rome?"

The answer to this question depends on WHEN you do, or did do, the counting. The following information may be helpful at this point. The ancient city of Rome was located on the left bank of the Tiber, and seven hills were named: *Palatine, Aventine, Caeline, Equiline, Viminal, Rimal, and Capitoline.*

As Rome grew in power and size, it took in another hill, Janiculum, which was also numbered among the seven hills, and the hill Capitoline was omitted. Still later another hill, *Pincian*, north of ancient Rome, was added, requiring the subtraction of one of the other hills."[89]

Consider Lynchburg Virginia

Even if we were all to agree that at some point in history, there were seven hills within the city limits of Rome, we must not overlook the fact that there are other cities in the world that also have seven hills. For example, there is a sign standing at the city limits of Lynchburg, Virginia, that identifies Lynchburg as the "City of Seven Hills!" Is it not possible that Lynchburg, Virginia could be the home of the harlot? Considering the animosity toward the late Jerry Falwell, the Moral Majority, and the mixing of politics and religion that took place during 1980's, some people would enjoy identifying Lynchburg with Babylon and Falwell as the Anti-Christ.

One Hill Left Standing

Most supporters of the traditional view overlook the fact that *the text specifically says that five of those mountains had ceased to exist when John wrote The Revelation.* If we establish the fact that Rome is the city of seven hills, then *Rome*

---

[89]John Walvoord, Prophecy Bible Handbook

cannot be the home of the harlot because when John wrote, there was only one "hill" standing. Consider the text says, not what interpreters would like it so say:

- **Five of these hills** had fallen by the time John wrote The Revelation.

- **One of those hills** was still standing when John wrote The Revelation.

- **One of those mountains** had not come into existence when John wrote (17:10).

The text is very clear. When John wrote The Revelation, he spoke of seven mountains which represented kings or rulers.

- **Five** of the seven mountains (rulers) had already disappeared.

- **One** of these mountains (rulers) was still standing (was still in existence when John wrote).

- **One mountain** (ruler/King) would rise in the future

The mountains were actually kings

Wouldn't a more accurate interpretation of the text be to realize that the mountains stand for kings. *They are not literal mountains. The mountains are symbolic for kings.*

We miss the point entirely when we waste our time trying to locate a city in which there are seven hills or mountains. The text solves the mystery itself in verse 10: *They are also seven kings!* The seven Mountains are actually seven political leaders or rulers of world empires.

Five Kings Were Gone

When John wrote from Patmos, only one of the seven mountains (kings) was standing (still ruling). The rest were gone.[90] If the mountains in the text were literal mountains instead of kings, then there would have been only *one mountain* left standing in the city of Rome, Italy, at the time of John's vision on Patmos.

One King Still Remained

One King (mountain) "was!" This means that, when John wrote, there was a one world empire and one supreme ruler. ***Obviously, the empire was Rome and the King was the Roman Emperor.***

One Future King

One King (mountain) John wrote about had not come upon the world scene at the time John was writing.   This *one "who has not yet come"* refers to a ruler who had not risen to power during John's day, but who will rise to power during the Tribulation period.

An Eighth King

John wrote also that there will also be an *eighth king* who would appear and rise to power in the latter days. Others have expressed doubts over whether the mountains in this chapter are literal hills in Rome, Italy.

---

[90]Egypt, Assyria, Babylon, Persia, & Greece had already fallen and had passed from history.

John Walvoord

On page 251 in his book, "The Revelation of Jesus Christ," John Walvoord reminds us: *"Thoughtful students of the Word know that is common in Scripture for the word mountain to refer to a kingdom, a regal dominion, or an established authority."*

"....the concept that the seven hills refer to the city of Rome is found to be unsupportable in the context, and the evidence that the city of Rome will be in some sense the Babylon represented here (Rev 17) does not have sufficient basis of support in other Scriptures to justify the conclusion." [91]

Walvoord recommends the following references for study regarding mountains being used as symbols for kings and rulers. (Psalm 30:7), (Jeremiah 51:25), and (Daniel 2:35).

Joseph Seiss

John Walvoord is not alone in questioning the traditional view of the seven hills referring to the city of Rome. He quotes Joseph A. Seiss on this matter on page 251, where he wrote: *"But a flimsier basis for such a controlling and all conditioning conclusion is perhaps no-where to be found. The seven hills of Rome, to begin with are <u>not mountains</u>, as everyone who has been there can testify, but the taking them as literal hills or mountains is founded upon a total misreading of the angels words."* ***If the hills represent kings, then do not refer to the seven hills of Rome and the whole conclusion that Rome is the capitol of ecclesiastical Babylon is brought into question."*** [92]

---

[91] John Walvoord, Prophecy Knowledge Handbook, (Wheaton: Victor Books, 1990) page 611
[92] Ibid. Page 608

Lehman Strauss

Writing in the Fall 1991 issue of "Word of Life" magazine, Dr. Lehman Strauss is quoted as saying: *"Now is this great harlot the Roman Catholic Church? The Great Harlot is called the Mother of Harlots (Rev 17:5). If she is the mother of harlots, her origin must be traced back beyond Romanism,* **for there was no Pope until the fourth century.** *The Roman Church is an old church, but certainly she is not the oldest church."*

Henry Morris

In his commentary on Revelation, Henry Morris gives additional light on this mystery. Morris said: *"But to say that Spiritual Babylon is either Rome or the Roman Catholic Church is to grossly underestimate the age-long global impact of this great mystery Babylon is the mother of all harlots and abominations of the earth. From her have come ancient paganism, Chinese Confucianism, Asian Buddhism, Indian Hinduism, Shamanism, Taoism, Shintoism, Animism, Astrology, Witch-craft, Spiritism, Sikhism, and all the worlds vast complex of gods and lords many."*[93]

Dr. C.I. Scofield

"It may well be that this union will embrace all the heathen religions of the world.

Vernon McGee

"The Great Harlot is that part of the church that will remain after the true church has been raptured. It will be composed of those who have never trusted Christ as their Savior. This is the group that enters the Great Tribulation."

---

[93]Henry Morris, <u>The Revelation Record</u> (Wheaton: Tyndale House Publishers, 1983), p 332

Oliver Greene

"This woman is not pagan Rome alone. She is the mother of every ism and false religion that has ever been born since Cain thought he could satisfy God with an offering of his own choosing. That takes in every church, every cult, religion, and church that does not give Christ and His verbally inspired Word preeminence in every detail of worship."

John Walvoord

"It becomes clear that Babylon in scripture is the name of a great system of religious error. Babylon is actually a counterfeit or pseudo religion which plagued Israel in the Old Testament as well as the church in the New Testament. Babylon is the source of counterfeit religion sometimes in the form of pseudo Christianity, sometimes in the form of pagan religion. It's most confusing form, however, is found in Romanism."[94]

ELEVEN FACTS ABOUT THE HARLOT AND THE BEAST SHE RIDES

The text mentions several interesting characteristics of this Great Harlot called Mystery Babylon. Read them and then ask yourself, "Does Rome really have all these characteristics?" You be the judge.

1. This woman is a Religious System.

The first thing we know about "Mystery Babylon" is that this woman is a religious system and the beast upon which she rides, is a political system.

---

[94]John Walvoord, <u>The Revelation of Jesus Christ</u> (Chicago: Moody Press, 1966) p 246.

2. This religious system is as old as Babylon.

The second thing we know about this religious system is that it is a very old system. In fact, it (she) is as old as ancient Babylon itself. This is where this woman came from.

3. This religious system is the source of all false Religion.

The religious system, which this woman represents, began in ancient Babylon and from there, spread through-out the world. She is called the "mother" of harlots, not the "daughter" of harlots. This suggests that she is the **source** of religious error, not the result of it.

4. This religions system has a world-wide influence.

The text mentions (17:15) that this harlot sits on many waters. *"And he saith unto me, The waters which thou sawest, where the harlot sitteth, **are peoples**, and multitudes, and nations, and tongues"*

The system of false religion this woman represents, began in ancient Babylon, and from there they spread to the rest of the world. Her evil doctrines have been embraced by men in every nation under heaven who have rejected the God of the Bible.

5. The Seven Heads Are Kings

In (Rev 17:9-10) we are told that the woman was riding on the back of a beast. This beast had seven heads. The writer identifies these "heads" as seven kings (world rulers). In the opinion of this writer, those five of these kings (who had fallen) were the rulers of the ancient kingdoms of **Egypt, Assyria, Babylon, Persia, and Greece.**

6. Five Kings Had Fallen

When John wrote The Revelation, five of these kings: Egypt, Assyria, Babylon, Persia, & Greece, had already fallen and disappeared from history.

7. One King Still Existed

The text says that "one king <u>was</u>." Doesn't this mean that one of these "kings" (mountains) was still in existence when John wrote The Revelation? **This "mountain" (King) can be none other than the Roman Empire itself**, because it was the world power when John wrote The Revelation. Therefore, we must conclude that the false religious beliefs of *Mystery Babylon* have been held in common by every heathen empire, from the time of ancient Babylon up until and including the Roman Empire.

8. This religious system is an idolatrous system

This false religious system, which began in Babylon and spread into the rest of the world is an Idolatrous system. It is a system that has turned the hearts of men and nations from the Living God to the worship of false religion.

9. The doctrines of this false system are seductive.

This woman who is riding the beast is very old, but she is still very attractive. She is so attractive that she will have the power to "seduce" the world rulers of all nations in the latter days. This promiscuous "lover" has seduced men of all ages and cultures. She has been "loved" by men in ancient times as well as the young humanist college professor in today's state universities.

10. This religious system is at war with Christianity.

This false religious belief is anti-Christian. The woman is said to be "drunk with the blood of the saints" (Rev 17:6). This woman is not only hostile toward God's people. She has murdered a great number of them over the centuries.

11. This woman imposes her false religion on the kings (rulers) of this world.

The text mentions that the *kings of the earth* have committed fornication with this woman (Rev 17:1-2). This means that rulers of every nation under heaven have followed the false religious beliefs this woman represents. She is seen in (17:3 & 7) as riding upon a scarlet beast. The angel explained that the heads of this beast are the rulers of the world empires of the past. (17:10-11).

12. The ten horns

The ten horns of the beast represent ten political leaders of the ten nation confederation that will rise to power during the tribulation. We must conclude that since this woman rides a beast which represents the world rulers of the past and future, she must represent a system of religious error that, for some reason, is appealing to political leaders. The text suggests that the political rulers *liked the woman* at first, but *hated here later and killed* her. This indicates that they liked her because they could "use" her. After she was no longer needed, she was destroyed (17:16).

THE BEAST REPRESENTS HUMAN GOVERNMENTS

1. The seven heads are **seven kings** not seven earthly mounds of rock and dirt.

2. These hills represent **kingdoms or empires** from the past, present, and the future.

3. **Five of the kings** (hills) had *already fallen*.They are" Egypt, Assyria, Babylon, Persia, and Greece.

4. **One king** (hill) was in existence when John wrote. That was clearly the Roman Empire.

5. **One king** (hill) was coming in the future. That mountain is the Anti- Christ.

6. **The ten horns are ten kingdoms.** These are the ten nations of the tribulation. One ruler will assume control over all ten.

John Walvoord, in his book, "Prophecy Knowlege Handbook," makes this interesting comment on this subject. *"The same ecclesiastical apostate church, typified by the woman that was supported and brought into being with the help of the political ruler, the scarlet beast, is now destroyed.*

The question is a natural one of how this fits into the sequence of events. In the overall picture of the last seven years leading up to the second coming of Christ, this passage indicates that in the first half of the seven years, this woman, representing the world religion, will have power, but probably will be a continuation of the world church movement in its present form from which the true church was raptured earlier in the sequence of events.

Now having come to the mid-point of the seven years when the head of the ten nations takes over as the world ruler, the apostate church is no longer useful and, as a matter of fact, is in the way. Accordingly, the ten nations destroy the woman and terminate her power and position."

The purpose behind this is that the world ruler will claim to be God himself, and for the final three-and-a-half years, the world religion will consist in the worship of the world ruler and the worship of Satan who is recognized to be the power behind the world ruler.

This is stated in Revelation 13:4 where the text says: "Men worshiped the Dragon because he had given authority to the Beast, and they also worshiped the beast saying, 'who is like the beast?' The whole religious system having its source in ancient Babylon is brought to its close because the final form of religion, the worship of the world ruler, is atheism, and does not need this support." [95]

---

[95]John Walvoord, Prophecy Knowledge Handbook, pages 609-610.

HOW COULD THIS POSSIBLY BE THE ROMAN CATHOLIC CHURCH?

In all honesty, how many of these characteristics can be found in the Roman Catholic Church? We would all agree that the Roman Catholic Church is a religious system. We will also agree that the Catholic Church is also a very old system, but not nearly old enough.

- Even if we agree with Hislop, and can trace many of the doctrines of Catholicism all the way back to Babylon, no honest historian believes that the Roman Catholic Church has existed since the days of the Babylonian empire.

- The Roman church may have been influenced by these false doctrines, but the **Roman Church is not the source of them.**

- Neither would any informed person imagine that the Catholic Church has influenced every world empire (Egypt, Assyria, Persia, Greece, and Rome) from Babylon to the present time.

- Is there any Catholic doctrine that has been held in common by the Assyrians, the Egyptians, the Babylonians, the Persians, the Greeks, and the Romans?

Granted, there are strong arguments to suggest that some Catholic doctrines border on idolatry. However, the great harlot represents a system that has turned the hearts of men and nations away from the living God to idolatry.

Does the Roman Catholic Church believe in the One True God and His Son Jesus Christ? The woman in Revelation 17 represents a movement that is totally anti-Christian and has shed the blood of believers down through the centuries.

- In all honesty, can one accuse the Catholic Church of being "Anti-Christian!

- Does the Catholic Church believe in Jehovah, the One True God?

- Do Catholics believe in the Virgin Birth of Jesus? Do Catholics believe in the Deity of Christ? Do Catholics believe in a literal heaven and hell?

- Although many liberal Protestants deny all of these doctrines, most good Catholics believe all of these.

ROME FAILS THE TEST

In the final analysis, the only evidence to support the traditional view that Rome is Mystery Babylon is the fact that some catholic practices and beliefs can be traced all the way back to Babylon. The traditional view fails every other test.

1. The Roman Catholic is not old enough.

2. The doctrines of the Roman Catholic Church have not been held by every world empire since Babylon.

3. The mountains in the text (Rev 17) are actually "kings," not hills in Italy or Virginia.

4. The doctrines of Rome might appeal to some, but they do not have universal appeal.

5. The Catholic Church does not reject the God of the Bible and His Son Jesus Christ.

6. The Roman Catholic doctrines are not "seductive" enough. If Rome is Mystery Babylon, then which of her doctrines has the world found so appealing? Is the veneration of Mary as "Queen of Heaven? Is it the practice of fasting for 40 days during Lent?

7. Is it the celebration of Easter or Christmas, which are undeniably of heathen origin?

8. Which of these doctrines have been in the world since the time of Babylon, which have been believed by every empire since then, which will be so appealing in the latter days that it will entice every false religious system in the world to merge into the giant super-church of the Tribulation?

9. The Unitarian church could qualify for "Mystery Babylon" much easier than the Catholic Church could, because the Unitarians deny nearly every basic Christian doctrine.

IS MYSTERY BABYLON = BABYLON?

The author's personal testimony

We were in the ministry for many years before we ever gave a "second thought" to Babylon, Iraq, or Islam. That has changed dramatically a few years ago when we were studying Eschatology at Luther Rice Seminary.

We had been given a writing assignment in which the professor gave the class a choice of topics from which we were to write a paper.

I looked over the list of topics and chose one I thought "would be a piece of cake." The topic I chose was "**Will Babylon be rebuilt?**"

This appeared to be a simple topic that would require a minimum of research. After all, *everybody knew* that Babylon had been destroyed in the days of Daniel and would *never* be rebuilt again. As far as we were concerned, Babylon was "history." It was a "done deal." As far as I was concerned, *the case was closed!*

The traditional view

Everything we had read up until this time taught that Babylon had already been destroyed; Babylon would never be inhabited again:

The Arabs will not even pitch their tents there.

No sheep-folds would be built there; animals will occupy the site.

The stones from the city of Babylon will not be taken away and used for other buildings, and men would not pass by the ruins of Babylon anymore.

Is "Babylon" really a code name for Rome?

In addition to this, most of us had been taught that "Babylon" was really a "code word" for "Rome." We had been taught that when Peter wrote the first epistle (1 Peter 5:13) he actually wrote from Rome, but he called it "Babylon." *The truth is, the Apostle Peter probably never saw the city of Rome in his life.*

References to Iraq in the Bible

I was totally unaware of the fact that there is more information in the Bible about Babylon and Iraq than there is about any other city other than Jerusalem. For example:

- **The Garden of Eden** was in Iraq (Genesis 2:10-14).

- **Adam & Eve** were created in Iraq (Genesis 2:7-8).

- **Satan** made his first recorded appearance in Iraq (Genesis 3:1-6).

- **Nimrod** established Babylon & Tower of Babel was built in Iraq (Gen. 10:8-97 & 11:1-4).

- **The confusion** of the languages took place in Iraq (Genesis 11:5-11).

- **Abraham** came from a city in Iraq (Genesis 11:31 &

Acts 7:2-4).

- **Isaac's bride,** Rebekka, came from Iraq (Gen. 24:3-4 & 10).

- **Jacob** spent 20 years in Iraq, working for his father-in-law (Gen. 27:42-45 & 31:38)

- **The greatest revival** in history was in a city in Iraq (Jonah 3).

- **Daniel** wrote from Iraq. That is where he was placed in the lion's den.

- **Iraq** is where the three Hebrew children were cast into the furnace of fire.

- **We also believe** that Babylon, in Iraq, will be the center of world commerce during the Tribulation.

Rejected traditional view

When I began to do a serious study on this subject, I experienced a rude awakening. I began to have serious reservations with the traditional position. I then rejected the traditional view totally and embraced a totally different interpretation. There is much evidence Mystery Babylon is literal Babylon itself.

1. Babylon is literal Babylon

Babylon is not a code word for Rome. When the Bible speaks of Babylon, it is referring to *literal Babylon*. Jacksonville is Jacksonville, Babylon is Babylon, and Rome is Rome.

2. Peter wrote from Babylon

Peter wrote his first epistle from the city of Babylon (Iraq), not Rome. *"The church that is at Babylon, elected together with you, greeteth you, and so doth Mark, my son." (1 Peter 5:13).* This writer doubts that the any credible *evidence* that the Apostle Peter ever set foot in the city of Rome.

3. Babylon was never destroyed

When Cyrus of Persia captured the city of Babylon in the days of Daniel, it happened so quietly and quickly that most of the city didn't even know it happened until three days later. The city was not totally destroyed. [96]

4. Alexander the Great

The city of Babylon was still flourishing in BC 331, when Alexander the Great approached the city. When he arrived at the gates, there was very little opposition. The inhabitants of Babylon opened the gates to him. Alexander was so pleased he actually helped them rebuild the temple of their idol, god, BEL.

5. Three Jewish Universities

In the fifth century, Theodoret reported that Babylon was inhabited by a large population of Jews. There were also three Jewish Universities in operation at that time. In the last year of the same century, the *Babylonian Talmud* was issued and recognized by Jews around the world.

---

[96] See Larkin: Book of Daniel, 1929, page 95.

6. The Stones of Babylon

The prophecy concerning final destruction of Babylon states that the stones of Babylon will not be used to build any more cities. *The truth of the matter is: The stones from Babylon have been used to build at least four other cities.* This means that the prophecies have not yet been fulfilled. Those prophecies are still future.

7. The late Saddam Hussein

Prior to the Gulf War, newspapers carried pictures of Saddam Hussein rebuilding the city with bricks bearing his name. Saddam dreamed of being the next Nebuchadnezzar.

8. Babylon's Judgment is Still Future

The destruction of Babylon that is described in chapters 16 and 18 of The Revelation are still future. We will address that subject in the latter part of this study.

9. Babylon will be rebuilt

Will Babylon be rebuilt? Babylon is being rebuilt right before our eyes.[97] One report stated: "Iraq under U.S. control has come further in six months than Germany did in seven years or Japan did in nine years following WWII."

10. A letter from Iraq (back in 2007)

"As I head off to Baghdad for the final weeks of my stay in Iraq, I wanted to say thanks to all of you who did not believe the media. They have done a very poor job of covering everything that has happened. . . .And just so you can rest at night knowing something is happening in Iraq that is noteworthy, I thought I

---

[97]This message was delivered in November 2004.

would pass this on to you. This is the list of things that has happened in Iraq recently: (He added: "Please share it with your friends and compare it to the version that your newspaper is producing.")"[98]

- Over 400,000 kids have up-to-date immunizations.

- School attendance is up 80% from levels before the war.

- Over 1,500 schools have been renovated and rid of the weapons stored there so education can occur.

- The country had its first 2 billion barrel export of oil in August.

- Over 4.5 million people have clean drinking water for the first time ever in Iraq.

- 100% of the hospitals are open and fully staffed, compared to 35% before the war.

- Sewer and water lines are installed in every major city.

- Over 60,000 police are patrolling the streets.

- Over 100,000 Iraqi civil defense police are securing the country.

- Over 80,000 Iraqi soldiers are patrolling the streets.

- Over 400,000 people have telephones for the first time ever.

---

[98]Ray Reynolds, SFC Iowa Army National Guard 234th Signal Battalion:

224

- Girls are allowed to attend school.

- Textbooks that don't mention Saddam are in the schools for the first time in 30 years.

11. A letter from a Marine (2007)[99]

- Saddam is gone, Iraq is free, and President Bush has not faltered or failed.

- Nearly all of Iraq's 400 courts are functioning.

- All 22 universities and 43 technical institutes and colleges are open.

- Teachers earn from 12 to 25 times their former salaries.

- All 240 hospitals and more than 1200 clinics are open.

- Doctors' salaries are at least eight times what they were under Saddam.

- Pharmaceutical distribution has gone from essentially nothing to 700 tons in May to a current total of 12,000 tons.

- 95 percent of all prewar bank customers have service and first-time customers are opening accounts daily.

- Iraqi banks are making loans to finance businesses.

- Iraq has one of the worlds' most growth-oriented investment and banking laws.

- Iraq has a single, unified currency for the first time in 15 years.

---

[99]From the Commanding Officer at MWSS-171 to his Marines.

- Satellite TV dishes are legal.

- There are more than 170 newspapers.

-

- Foreign journalists (and everyone else) are free to come and go.

- In Baghdad alone residents have selected 88 advisory councils.

- Baghdad's first democratic transfer of power in 35 years happened when the city council elected its new chairman.

Will Babylon be rebuilt? Babylon is being rebuilt before our very eyes.

JOEL ROSENBERG

Some of the most fascinating information about the rebuilding of Babylon is found in the book *Epicenter*, by Joel Rosenberg.[100] Rosenberg predicts:

1. Iraq will emerge as the wealthiest country in the Middle East,

2. Iraq will become the oil superpower.

3. The prophets Ezekiel, Isaiah, and Daniel, all picture Babylon as a city of wealth and power.

4. People will marvel at the wealth of gold, silver, and pearls (Rev. 18:12).

5. Iraq will survive because she will not be in involved when Russia, Iran, and the Arab nations come down to

---

[100]Joel Rosenberg, Epicenter (Carol Stream, Illinois: Tyndale House, 2006)

attack Israel (Ezekiel 38-39).

6. Voter turnout is better in Iraq than in Gainesville, Florida.[101] Iraq had a 58% turn out in January 2005; 63% turned out in October of 2005; and 77% turned out in December of 2005.[102]

7. Iraq's economy has nearly doubled since the liberation. It grew 10.4% in 2006 and 15.5% in 2007.

8. Inflation in Iraq has dropped from 32% down to 10% (page 181).

9. Visa opened for business in Babylon in 2003.

10. Fed Ex began house-to-house pickups in Bagdad, Basra, and Mosul (Ninevah) in August 2003 (page 178).

11. In 2003, Coco-Cola, which had been banned from Iraq under Sadaam (because they did business with Israel) has entered into a contract and beat Pepsi, their arch competitor (page 181).

12. In December of 2003, The Wall Street Journal featured an article titled "Iraq! Open for Business."

13. Several large companies have entered the market in Iraq. Among them are GM, Nokia, Lucent, Motorola, and Canon (182).

14. 33,000 new businesses have been registered in Iraq.

15. 1.5 million people have been employed to rebuild schools, hospitals, etc.

What others have said

This present writer is not the only person to have reservations about the traditional view that Babylon had

---

[101]Gene Keith made this observation.
[102]Page 179

already been destroyed and would never be inhabited again. It was only after we had completed our research that we discovered that several other writers we admire had come to the same conclusions. For example:

Vernon McGee

"There has been some disagreement upon conservative expositors about whether or not ancient Babylon will be rebuilt. Candidly, for many years I took that position that it would not be rebuilt. However, I believe now it will be rebuilt."[103]

"I personally believe that Mystery Babylon is Rome and that, when it goes down in the midst of the Tribulation, the religious center shifts to Jerusalem because that is where the False Prophet will put up the image of the Anti-Christ to be worshiped. Commercial Babylon is ancient Babylon, rebuilt as the commercial capital of the world. This city will be the final capital of the political power of the Beast."[104]

Henry Morris

"Zechariah's vision thus clearly foretells a time when the center of world finance and commerce will be removed from its' bases in New York, Geneva, and other great cities and transported quickly across the world to a new foundation and headquarters in the land of Shinar. The land of Shinar, of course, is simply a biblical term for Babylon, and has been since Babel was erected there."[105]

There is no question in our minds about the fact that Iraq will become a major player in the Middle East. And it is

---

[103]Vernon McGee, Thru the Bible, (Nashville: Thomas Nelson, 1983) Vol. V, page 1037.
    [104]McGee, page 1036
    [105]Henry Morris, commenting on Zechariah 5:5-11) (book missing) p 355

our firm belief that Babylon will become the center of commerce during the Tribulation and the final days of history.

Vernon McGee

"Babylon is the headquarters of demons and has been down through the years. . . . This indicates that Babylon is where demons of the spirit and unclean birds of the natural world will be incarcerated during the Millennium" (Isaiah 13L19-22) (Jeremiah 50:38-40).

John Walvoord

"Babylon will be the prison (holding cage) of every evil spirit, fallen angel, and demon during the Millennium."[106]

Henry Morris

"There will be a swarm of unclean birds fouling the ruins, feasting on the charred flesh of the inhabitants.

These may well be from the great flocks following the armies of the East trooping across the dried up Euphrates (Rev. 16:12).

God has bidden them to the great supper of Armageddon (Rev. 19:17-18), just as they feasted on the armies of God and Magog in Israel seven years earlier (Ezekiel 39:17-20).

These unclean birds will gladly postpone their westward flight in order to perch in the ruins of Babylon for a time." [107]

World Commercial Center

Very few people seem to realize that Babylon will become

---

[106]Walvoord, page 259.
[107]Henry Morris, The Revelation Record, page 353

the political and commercial center of the entire world during the Tribulation.

Vernon McGee

Vernon McGee makes an interesting comment on this. *"If a small nation in the mid-east can turn off the spigot to stop the flow of oil and bring the world to its knees, what will it be like when ancient Babylon in that very area becomes again the world center." "New York City will become a whistle stop on the Tonerville Trolley. . . . Los Angles will return to an adobe village. London and other great cities will become mere villages with muddy streets."* [108]

Joel Rosenberg

Joel Rosenberg predicts that Iraq will become the oil superpower of the Middle East. Every serious student of prophecy must read Rosenberg's book, *Epicenter*. Read what Rosenberg wrote about Iraq's oil reserves on page 182. Read what a Congressional Research Survey concluded (183).

1. Iraq: The Future Oil Superpower

When Russia, Iraq, and other Arab countries attack Israel in the battle of Gog and Magog (Ezekiel 38-39), Russia and her allies will be annihilated. Iraq will survive because she is not in that Mideast coalition.

Joel Rosenberg predicts: *"Oil and gas exports from those countries will be slowed or halted altogether because of the terrible destruction described by Ezekiel. Iraq, meanwhile, as one of the few Middle Eastern countries not having participated in the attack on Israel, will become one of the few oil powers (besides*

---

[108]McGee, Vol. V. Page 1043.

Israel) left intact when the smoke clears. As oil and gas prices skyrocket due to severe shortages, the world will become increasingly dependent upon Iraq for energy, and money will flow into their coffers as never before." [109]

Iraq: Magnet for World Banking

Joel Rosenberg predicts:[110] *"In short order, Iraq will emerge as an oil super-power rivaling Saudi Arabia. Trillions of petro-dollars will flood into the country.*

As this happens, Iraq will become a magnet for banks and multinational corporations that will set up the regional and multinational headquarters in that country. High-rise office buildings, luxury apartments, and single-family homes will be constructed. Theaters, concert halls, parks and malls will be built.

The ancient city of Babylon will emerge virtually overnight like a phoenix rising from the ashes, to become one of the modern wonders of the world."

[109] Joel Rosenberg, Epicenter (Carol Stream Illinois: Tyndale House: 2006) p 174.
[110] Page 173

IS MYSTERY BABYLON MECCA?

Walid Shoebat

Last week (November 2013), while I was editing this book, (originally written in 2007 and updated in December 2013), I came across an article by a man named Walid Shoebat that really grabbed my attention. I don't know very much about Shoebat except that he was born in Bethlehem, is a converted Muslim, and a very controversial Bible teacher. However, Shoebat gave some interesting thoughts about Mystery Babylon we would for you to consider.

Walid Shoebat believes that Mystery Babylon is not Rome, nor Babylon, but Mecca, the home of the Kaaba and the holiest site in the world for Muslims. He provides some impressive evidence for his position.

We have included the following remarks from his May 31, 2013 blog. You can check out his article on the following website. Please! Check it out. **(Used by permission)**

http://shoebat.com/2013/05/31/mystery-babylon-is-mecca-not-vatican/

"When it comes to Mystery Babylon, the common tendency amongst many Protestant theologians is to liken it to Rome. According to them, Rome is the city of seven hills. Others even equate it with Iraq, since this was home to the original Babylon.

Years ago, many books were written about Saddam Hussein, who was allegedly hard at work, rebuilding Babylon. Christians gobbled up the books without truly examining the evidence. Saddam was simply rebuilding a tourist attraction where Nineveh once stood, the project was later abandoned and Saddam died on the gallows along with the prophecy books that included his name.

But when presenting a multitude of biblical evidence, people still angrily deny this interpretation because they have etched in their minds a verse or two insisting it's still Rome, while *adhering to a centuries-old theory initiated by Martin Luther. That plus today's Catholics do not bite. In fact, a clue to the real Babylon was just presented in an article by Aaron Klein when he stated this week that:*

"Forces in the Persian Gulf and Arab intelligence services have noted the establishment of Iranian missile launch sites aimed in the direction of Saudi Arabia and Qatar, according to Egyptian and Jordanian intelligence officials speaking to WND."

Yet, no one in the prophecy arena has even raised a single red flag about the significance of this report; Iran (biblical Elam) must destroy Arabia.

In Isaiah 21:9, Isaiah levels a prophetic oracle against Babylon using the same announcement in Revelation 18:1-2 and Revelation 14:8: "Babylon is fallen, is fallen":

*"The burden against **Dumah**" (Isaiah 21:11)*

*"The burden against **Arabia**" (Isaiah 21:13)*

*"All the glory of **Kedar** will fail" (Isaiah 21:16)*

These are all in Arabia, which is destroyed by Iran "Elam" (Isaiah 21:2)
There has been an immense oversight by many in the field of biblical eschatology; that when it comes to the destruction of end-days Babylon,

*Scripture makes no mention of any of the ancient Babylonian cities: Nineveh, Ur, Babel, Erech, Accad, Sumer, Assur, Calneh, Mari, Karana, Ellpi, Eridu, Kish, or Tikrit. **All of the literal references in Scripture are in Arabia**.*

*The use **"MOTHER OF HARLOTS"**, while it is commonly attributed to the Vatican's Mariology with the worship of Ishtar, history records that the worship of Ishtar "Kilili", or "Queen of Harlots" [1] originated from Arabia, not Rome.*

In fact, when Muslims roam roundabout the black stone, it is a throwback to the worship of Ishtar, whom they called Athtar and Allat.

When it comes to the Harlot woman, the Kaaba is a perfect match. The black tarp is considered by Muslims to be a woman's dress (Kiswa) as Edward Gibbons elaborated:

"...the kuswa of the magnificent Kaaba, is what is used for clothing of a [virtuous] covering, on top of it, it is written, the Kaaba's dressing, meaning 'we have dressed her her dress." [2]

Everything that the harlot is described it fits the Ka'ba; dress, pearls, jewels, gold, silver and even the blasphemies etched in silver threads with golden inlays across her attire. Just the doors of the Ka'ba alone has 280 kilograms of pure gold.

The reference to a prostitute in Revelation 17 regarding the "Whore of Babylon" is no coincidence:

"And the woman (whore) was arrayed in purple and scarlet color" (v. 17)...

...resembles the near copulating with the Ka'ba's Black Stone, which historically was dedicated to Aphrodite, the prostitute goddess that was called "Aphrodite Porne" (Aphrodite the Prostitute), "the goddess adorned in purple", similar to the depictions given in Revelation 17:4, which the Ka'ba has a scarlet-colored inner garment. John of Damascus notes:

"After the Hajj was performed by Muhammad, the 'rubbing and kissing the [of the Black Stone]...was extremely passionate.'"

Muslim tradition even perpetuates the blasphemy that: "Abraham had sexual intercourse with Hagar on it" (Sahas. Heresy, Pages 88-89).

Francis Burton writes regarding the Ka'ba: *"the part of the cover (Kiswa), covering the door, is called [a Burka] just like the veil the Arabic women are wearing in front of their face...in fact,*

Arab mystics even compare the Ka'ba to a virgin, adorned with her finest wedding dress." (Vol 3, page 295)

Even today during their Hajj pilgrimage, Muslims kiss, rub and caress the Black Rock.

Furthermore, it is impossible to even consider that Isaiah 21 was referring to an historic battle between Persia and ancient Babylon since the multiple references throughout are not connected to ancient Iraq but to Kedar, Tema, Dedan and Dumah, which are all in Saudi Arabia near Yathrib (Medina), and today is known as "Dumat el-Jandal." Dumah, one of the sons of Ishmael, is also associated with Edom and Seir in Isaiah 21:11. It is believed by many that Kedar, Ishmael's son, is the line from which Muhammad descended.

Even Muslims recognize when they read Isaiah 21, they see Isaiah 21:14-15 as the story of Muhammad when the Muslims emigrated from Mecca to Medina (Tema) in which they were fed and rescued from the sword. No westerner was able to interpret:

"The inhabitants of the land of Tema brought water to him that was thirsty, they prevented with their bread him that fled. For they fled from the swords, from the drawn sword, and from the bent bow, and from the grievousness of war." (Isaiah 21:14-15)

The Bible depicts that in this time, it will not be like the time when Muhammad fled; all Arabia – including the Glory of Kedar (Mecca) – will be destroyed. How else can anyone interpret:

"No Arab will pitch his tent there, no shepherd will rest his flocks there" (Isaiah 13:20)

Arabs pitch tents in Arabia, not Rome. *The ultimate fulfillment of this verse is the destruction of the Last-Days Babylon. We know this because the passage speaks about: "the*

237

day of the Lord" (v. 9) with the "heavens not giving light" (v. 10). This is not historical, but End-Times related.

Then we have the Red Sea: "The earth is moved at the noise of their fall, at the cry the noise thereof was heard in the Red sea." (Jeremiah 49:21)

The Red Sea is a geographic indicator as to where the Last-Days Babylon will be located.

Look at Mecca on any map and you will see that it sits near the Red Sea.

Some may object, saying that Jeremiah 49 is speaking about Edom, which was primarily located in modern day Jordan. Yet, in Ezekiel 25, "Edom" stretches from Teman (Yemen) to Dedan (Saudi Arabia)" (v. 13). Greater Edom included all of the west coast of the Arabian Peninsula.

Notice the description of her destruction: *"'As Sodom and Gomorrah were overthrown, along with their neighboring towns,' says the LORD, 'so no one will live there; no man will dwell in it,'" (Jeremiah 49:18).*

It is no surprise that Iran is focused on Saudi Arabia, since the Bible predicted that the harlot is destroyed by the beast she rides, that is, the nations she deceived with her spiritual harlotry — Islam.

[1] Patricia Turner and Charles Russell Coulter, Dictionary of Ancient Deities, Page 242, Ishtar, Oxford University Press US, 2001.

[2] Edward Gibbon, The Decline and Fall of The Roman Empire, Volume 6, Chap. 1, Page 211., Little, Brown, and Company, 1855.

Be sure to go to his website and take the time to watch the video which describes in detail the "clothing" for the black stone in Mecca. **(Used by permission)**

http://shoebat.com/2013/05/31/mystery-babylon-is-mecca-not-vatican/

END OF QUOTES FROM WALID SHOBAT

IT'S TIME TO TAKE AN HONEST LOOK AT ISLAM

Are Allah and Jehovah the same God?

A majority of Americans claim to believe in God. This sounds good, but isn't it fair to ask: *"Which God do you believe in?* Someone will say: *"Well, it doesn't really matter, because we are all worshiping the same God."* Are we all worshiping the same God?

If we stood at the entrance of the Mall and took a survey and asked the question: "Who is Allah?" Here are some of the answers we might expect to receive:

Some would say, *"Allah is the name for God used by the followers of Mohammad."*

Others might say: *"Allah is just another name for the same God Christians and Jews call Jehovah.*

They would tell us that Muslims, Jews, and Christians all worship the same God, they just call him by another name. If that is what you think - you are in for a startling discovery.

Allah and Jehovah are two separate beings. Allah and Jehovah are as different as night is from day. Allah is as different from Jehovah as the god the Mormons worship.

239

Allah is as different from Jehovah as the god the Masons worship.

A critical issue

This is a very critical issue. And that is correct. There are five (5) "Pillars" of Islam. The very first of these five pillars is: *There is no God but Allah, and Muhammad is his messenger."* The Bible says the same thing about Jehovah. The very First Commandment establishes the fact that there is only One True and living God (Exodus 20:1-2). *"And God spake all these words, saying, I am the LORD thy God, which have brought thee out of the land of Egypt, out of the house of bondage. Thou shalt have no other gods before me."*

Who is Allah?

Would you please take a few minutes of your time to see if we can find out who Allah really is? If Allah is just another name for Jehovah, we need to know it. If, however, Allah and Jehovah are two separate beings, then we need to know that too.

Background

Allah is the god of Islam. The word "Islam" in Arabic means "submission." A Muslim is one who submits to Allah. Mohammad is the founder of the religion of Islam. Mohammad, the founder of Islam, was born in 570 A.D. and died at the age of 62 (632).

Camel Driver

Mohammad was a camel driver until the age of 25 when he married an older woman who was quite wealthy. For the next 15 years, Mohammad and his wife ran a fruit business.

Cave Experiences

When Mohammad was 40 years old he began going into a cave to meditate. This cave was about three miles north of Mecca. While he was praying and meditating in that cave, Mohammad would go into, what some describe as epileptic seizures (fits). He would shake; he would perspire, and he would foam at the mouth. Some believe he suffered from epilepsy. Others believe Mohammad was experiencing demon possession.

Visited by Gabriel

According to Muslim tradition, while Mohammad was meditating in that cave near Mecca, the angel Gabriel appeared to Mohammad and gave him several special revelations.

The Koran

Those revelations were not written down in a book called the "Koran" until years later because Mohammad was *uneducated and probably did not know how to read or write.* Among those revelations Mohammed received are:

1. Allah was the *one true god.* He created everything.

2. Man is *God's slave.* Man's chief duty is to submit to god. That's what the word "Islam" means: submission.

3. There will be a day of judgment. Man will be saved or lost depending on his good deeds (works).

4. Gabriel also told Mohammad that he was to *loot and steal* from the caravans that were passing through and that he

was to *kill the men.*

5. The Koran reports that Mohammad fought many battles and killed tens of thousands of people.

6. Gabriel also told Mohammad to *kill and drive out all Jews.* At one time Mohammad caught 1,000 Jewish men, brought them together, and had them beheaded.

7. In another revelation, Gabriel told Mohammad that Islam was to be exalted above all other religions, including Judaism and Christianity.

8. This is why Islam is known the world over as "*The Religion of the Sword.*"

9. Today, approximately 1/6 of the world's population practices this religion. **Who is this Allah that is worshiped by 1/6 of the world's population? You will be startled to find out**.

Animistic Culture

In ancient Arabia, long before Mohammad was born, the culture was "animistic." Every Arab tribe had its sacred, magic stones, which the Arabians believed, protected their tribes. Mohammad's tribe had adopted "a black stone." This stone was probably an asteroid or a meteorite that had fallen from heaven and the *Arabs believed it to be divine.*

Sabianism

The dominant religion of that day was "Sabianism," which was the worship of the sun, moon, and stars.

Moon worship

The Arabs believed the moon was a *male deity*, and a lunar calendar was used. Their pagan fasting would begin on the crescent moon.

Mohammad's Tribe

Allah was the moon god and he was represented by the black stone that had come down from heaven. Allah (moon god) was worshiped by the Arabs long before Mohammad came along.

The Sun god

The Arabs of that day also believed the sun was the female goddess. They believed that Allah, the moon god married the sun goddess, and they gave birth to the 3 daughters of Allah.

360 gods

When Mohammad came along, there were 360 different gods worshiped by the Arabians and moon and the sun topped the list. When Mohammad took control of Mecca, he destroyed all of the idols except one: Allah, the moon god, who was represented by the black stone.

The Crescent Moon

In the days before Islam, the symbol of the moon god, Allah, was the crescent. It was common throughout the Middle East today. The crescent moon can be seen on every Islamic flag, in every Mosque, and even on the hats of men who belong to the Order of the Mystic Shrine.

The order of the Mystic Shrine

Have you ever seen a parade where members of the Shrine Club were present and were driving their funny cars? Did you look closely at those hats they were wearing? Do you have any idea what those hats stand for and where those symbols came from? They are called "Fezes," and were named after a city named Fez.

Many years ago (8th century) in Morocco, there was a Christian community named Fez. One day, a horde of Muslim (terrorists) swooped down upon that Christian community and *murdered ever Christian in the city.* The Muslim raiders were shouting *"There is no god but Allah and Muhammad is his prophet."*

These devout Muslims literally *butchered* every born-again Christian in that city. During the butchering of the people of Fez, the streets literally ran red with *the blood of martyred Christians.* The Muslim murderers dipped their caps in the blood of their victims as a testimony to Allah. Those blood stained caps eventually were called "fezzes" *and became a badge of honor for those who killed a Christian.* Today, members of the Shrine Club wear that same fez today, with the Islamic sword and crescent encrusted with jewels. The tragedy is - many are worn by men who profess to be Christians themselves. According to Muslim law, there is mandatory death penalty for anyone who defiles the name of the Islamic prophet Mohammad.[111]

Allah and the Order of the Mystic Shrine

Did you know that, when a member of the *Order of the Mystic Shrine* is initiated at the Alter of Obligation, he must bow in worship, with his hands tied behind his back, and

---

[111]Gainesville Sun, Saturday, May 9, 1998.

proclaim Allah (the demon god) to be the god of his fathers.

Members of the Order of the Mystic Shrine take a blood oath and confess that Allah is God.

This fact is documented in the secret lodge document, *THE MYSTIC SHRINE*: An Illustrated Ritual of the Ancient Arabic Order of Nobles of the Shrine, 1975 edition (pages 20-22).[112]

Muslims kill Christians

Now, back to the possibility that Islam could possibly be the most powerful force in the one-world apostate religious system of the Tribulation, consider the fact that Muslims are already killing God's people all over the world today.

- **Pakistan:** At the time of this writing (2007) there were 200 Christians awaiting death in Pakistan. They have been sentenced to death for "blasphemy."

- **Saudi Arabia:** In Saudi Arabia, two pastors were beheaded because they dared to hold a Bible study[113]

- **East Java:** In East Java, a crowd of 10,000 Muslims attacked tore down and burned the home of a Christian preacher, to protest the tracts he had

---

[112]Carlson & Decker, "Fast Facts about False Teachings," Eugene, Oregon: Harvest House. 1994.

[113] Associated Press, Feb. 8, 1993. Carlson & Decker, "Fast Facts on False Teachings." Eugene , Oregon: Harvest House, 1994, page 103.

distributed.[114]

- **Gulf War:** During the Gulf War, chaplains in the US military were not allowed to wear their tiny crosses on their lapels. Service men were told to leave their Bibles at home.

- **Islamic law forbids** even the presence or even the mention of Christianity on "Muslim" soil.

---

[114]Washington Post, Jan. 3, 1993

SUMMARY

Is there any religion in the world today that has all of the characteristics listed in the text?

1. Islam is a false religion. Allah is the "moon god" of pagan Arabs.[115]

2. Islam hates Christianity, calls Christians and Jews "infidels," and kills them today.

3. Islam believes in forced conversion.

4. Islam is more than a religion. It is also a system of government.

5. Islam is reported to be the fastest growing religion in the world, especially in American prisons.

6. When all true believers are removed from the earth prior to the tribulation, there will no power on earth to prevent Islam from taking over the whole (lost) world.

7. Muslims hate Israel and refuse to even acknowledge her right to exist.

8. Islam is seductive. It is attracting young militants from all over the world (even in America).

---

[115] See article, "who is Allah," by Gene Keith

9. There is no other religion on earth that even comes close to Islam in fitting the description in The Revelation.

10. In ten years (2017), 50 percent of the Russian military will be Muslims.

We believe that Islam is definitely false religious system that will "head up" the apostate religious system of the Great Tribulation.

Vernon McGee said: "*The Great Harlot is that part of the church that will remain after the true church has been raptured. It will be composed of those who have never trusted Christ as their Savior. This is the group that enters the Great Tribulation.*"

- All Atheists will be left behind.

- All unsaved members from every church and from every denomination.

- All unsaved pastors, priests, and popes.

- All Pantheists who worship nature and "mother earth."

- All Polytheist who worship many gods.

- All unsaved Evolutionist who have rejected God as creator and worship the god of junk science and believe everything in the universe (matter, plant life, animal life, and man) are the result of the great scientific formula: Nothing x Time x Chance = Everything!

- All Animist and Spiritist who communicate with demons who pose as "spirit guides."

- All who believe in Astrology and worship the zodiac and believe the heavenly bodies (stars, etc.) control events on earth.

- All unsaved Humanist who dethrone God and exalt man.

- The millions of people who blindly follow the religious systems of the world.

- All unsaved Masons, Knights of Columbus, and members of the Order of the Mystic Shrine.

- All unsaved Mormons.

- All of the unsaved members of the various cults.

- All of these people will be left behind when Christ comes for His Church. At that point, they will all come together and form a one-world religion.

- All devout Muslims who worship Allah and hate Christians and Jews, who convert with the sword.

WHERE IS MYSTERY BABYLON?

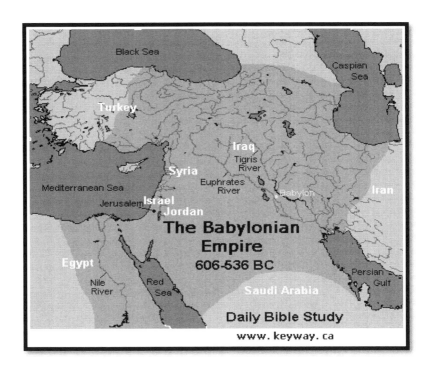

Look closely at this picture. This is a map of the ancient Babylonian Empire. That area is Muslim country today. Doesn't it make sense to conclude that this is MYSTERY BABYLON?

A WOMAN RIDING A BEAST

(Picture courtesy of Google images)

The monument in the picture above stands in front of the European Union build in Brussels. Are we seeing prophecy fulfilled before our very eyes?

SELF TEST

Let's take a moment out and see how you score on the following quiz. The question is: **"What religion or earth today seeks to control every person, every city, every state, and every continent, and plans to kill those who refuse to submit?**

Check the correct answer.

( ) Roman Catholic
( ) United Methodist
( ) Southern Baptist
( ) Pentecostal
( ) Islam

It doesn't take a rocket scientist to understand that Islam is the only religious movement in the world today that can qualify as the Harlot riding the Beast. *It's a no brainer!*

Dr. Erwin Lutzer

For those of you who may not be my not be familiar with Islam and Sharia, let us share a paragraph or two from Dr. Erwin Lutzer's book, *The Cross in the Shadow of the Crescent.*

"What is shariah? Perhaps you've heard the term before, and you know it has something to do with Islamic law. Before we can go any further, it's vital to have a clear understanding of shariah, for it explains much of what we need to know about Islam.

One resource defines shariah this way: Translated as "the path," shariah is a comprehensive legal and political framework. Though it certainly has spiritual elements, it would be a mistake to think of shariah as a 'religious' code in the Western sense because it seeks to regulate all manner of behavior in the secular sphere— economic, social, military, legal, and political." (*Lutzer, Erwin W. (2013-02-01). The Cross in the Shadow of the Crescent (p. 32). Harvest House Publishers. Kindle Edition.*)

"What is it that makes shariah so dangerous to Western society? At first glance, we might think there is no harm in permitting Muslims to observe shariah within their own communities, which already happens right now in Europe and the United Kingdom. But shariah is viewed as being sacred and coming from Allah himself, which, in the adherents' eyes, makes it superior to all other law systems: [Muslim writers who subscribe to the supreme authority of shariah over all other laws] teach that since everything in the universe belongs to Allah, and as Muslims are the true followers of Allah and therefore his rightful representatives, the oversight of the earth— especially the exercise of political power or authority— is the responsibility of Muslims. All others are usurpers from whom Muslims must endeavor to take power. (*Ibid page 34)*

PS Mecca is also a city of seven hills. They are: Jabal abu Siba', Jabal Safa, Jabal Marwah, Jabal abu Milhah, Jabal abu Ma'aya, Jabal abu Hulayah and Jabal abu Ghuzlan.

(http://www.omegaletter.com/articles/articles.asp?ArticleID=7770)

CHAPTER 18

THE FINAL DESTRUCTION OF BABYLON

There are two Babylons in chapters 17 & 18. One is a religious system and the other is a commercial system.

The religious system appears as a harlot riding on the back of a scarlet colored beast. She is called "Mystery Babylon, the Mother of harlots."

The commercial system is portrayed as the beast upon which this woman rides and it is called "Babylon the Great."

Both of these systems are evil and they will rise to power during the Great Tribulation.

Both of them will also be destroyed during the Tribulation.

The Harlot (the false religious system) will be destroyed.

The beast (the commercial system) will be destroyed at the end of the Tribulation.

Where is this city? Is it in Iraq? Is it Rome? Is it the United States? Is it Mecca?   Wherever it is, it is going to be destroyed.

(Rev. 18:3) *"For all the nations have drunk of the wine of the wrath of her fornication, the* **kings**[116] *of the earth have committed fornication with her, and the* **merchants**[117] *of the earth have become rich through the abundance of her luxury."*

Politicians and power brokers had become wealthy as the result of government contracts, pork barrel projects and under-the-table business deals.

God's last call (Rev. 18:4)

"Then I heard another voice from heaven saying, "Come out of her, my people, lest you share in her sins, and lest you receive of her plagues. This is God's last call to any believers who are not a part of this corrupt system and want to escape before destruction. Some wonder how there can still be any saved people left or why they would even be there. Just

---

[116]Politicians (McGee, page 1037)

[117]Literally "Those who travel." (Brokers perhaps?)

think about it.

Vernon McGee reminds us that business is one of the biggest excuses men have for not having time for God. Think of the Rich Young Ruler. Think of the farmer God called a fool. Think of Lot living in Sodom. God had to send angels to drag Lot out before the cities were destroyed by fire and brimstone. *Why was Lot living in Sodom in the first place?*

Babylon's sins stink (Rev. 18:5-7)

5 For her sins have reached to heaven, and God has remembered her iniquities.

6 Render to her just as she rendered to you, and repay her double according to her works; in the cup which she has mixed, mix double for her.

7 In the measure that she glorified herself and lived luxuriously, in the same measure give her torment and sorrow; for she says in her heart, 'I sit as queen, and am no widow, and will not see sorrow.'

8 Therefore her plagues will come in one day--death and mourning and famine. And she will be utterly burned with fire, for strong is the Lord God who judges her."

Politicians and financiers will weep (Rev. 18:9-17)

9 "The kings (politicians) of the earth who committed fornication and lived luxuriously with her will weep and lament for her, when they see the smoke of her burning,

10 standing at a distance for fear of her torment, saying, 'Alas, alas, that great city Babylon, that mighty city! For in one hour your judgment has come.'

11 And the merchants of the earth will weep and mourn over her, for no one buys their merchandise anymore:

12 *merchandise of gold and silver, precious stones and pearls, fine linen and purple, silk and scarlet, every kind of citron wood, every kind of object of ivory, every kind of object of most precious wood, bronze, iron, and marble;*

13 *and cinnamon and incense, fragrant oil and frankincense, wine and oil, fine flour and wheat, cattle and sheep, horses and chariots, and bodies and* souls of men.

14 *The fruit that your soul longed for has gone from you, and all the things which are rich and splendid have gone from you, and you shall find them no more at all.*

15 *The merchants of these things, who became rich by her, will stand at a distance for fear of her torment, weeping and wailing,*

16 *and saying, 'Alas, alas, that great city that was clothed in fine linen, purple, and scarlet, and adorned with gold and precious stones and pearls!*

17 *For in one hour such great riches came to nothing.'*

Shipping magnates will weep (Rev. 18:18-19)

18 Every ship-master, all who travel by ship, sailors, and as many as trade on the sea, stood at a distance

18 and cried out when they saw the smoke of her burning, saying, 'What is like this great city?'

19 They threw dust on their heads and cried out, weeping and wailing, and saying, 'Alas, alas, that great city, in which all who had ships on the sea became rich by her wealth! For in one hour she is made desolate.'

Notice the reference to ship-masters, sailors, and those who trade by sea. Babylon will be the commercial center of the world. Could this be a reference to the many oil tankers and cargo ships that will be carrying oil from Iraq and goods to Iraq from other nations?

Babylon will eventually be destroyed (Rev. 18:20-24)

20 Rejoice over her, O heaven, and you holy apostles and prophets, for God has avenged you on her!"

21 Then a mighty angel took up a stone like a great millstone and threw it into the sea, saying, "Thus with violence the great city Babylon shall be thrown down, and shall not be found anymore.

22 The sound of harpists, musicians, flutists, and trumpeters shall not be heard in you anymore. No craftsman of any craft shall be found in you anymore, and the sound of a millstone shall not be heard in you anymore.

23 The light of a lamp shall not shine in you anymore, and the voice of bridegroom and bride shall not be heard in you anymore. For your merchants were the great men of the earth, for by your sorcery all the nations were deceived.

24 And in her was found the blood of prophets and saints, and of all who were slain on the earth."

Harmful associations

Men always have some excuse for compromising and being involved with harmful associations. Some of the (saved) people involved in the commercial activities of Babylon probably used the excuse, "We need to be here as witnesses."

Isaiah 13:19-22.

The destruction of Babylon will take place in the period called "The day of the Lord." On that great day, stars will fall, the sun and moon will be darkened.

[19]And Babylon, the glory of kingdoms, the beauty of the Chaldees' excellency, shall be as when God overthrew Sodom and Gomorrah.

20It shall never be inhabited, neither shall it be dwelt in from generation to generation: neither shall the Arabian pitch tent there; neither shall the shepherds make their fold there.

21But wild beasts of the desert shall lie there; and their houses shall be full of doleful creatures; and owls shall dwell there, and satyrs shall dance there.

22And the wild beasts of the islands shall cry in their desolate houses, and dragons in their pleasant palaces: and her time is near to come, and her days shall not be prolonged."

Jeremiah 50:40

Jeremiah prophesied that the destruction of Babylon will be like the destruction of Sodom and Gomorrah. It will be permanent!!

No one will ever live there again. *"As God overthrew Sodom and Gomorrah and the neighbor cities thereof, saith the LORD; so shall no man abide there, neither shall any son of man dwell therein."*

Jeremiah 51:43

Jeremiah also predicted that when Babylon is finally destroyed, no will ever live there again; Babylon will become a wilderness; nobody will ever pass by those ruins again. **This prophecy is still future.** *"Her cities are a desolation, a dry land, and a wilderness, a land wherein no man dwelleth, neither doth any son of man pass thereby."*

Jeremiah 51:26

When Babylon is finally destroyed, the stones from the city will not be moved or used to build any other cities. **This has not happened yet.** *And they shall not take of thee a stone for a corner, nor a stone for foundations; but thou shalt be*

261

desolate for ever, saith the LORD."

Revelation 16:17-19

John prophesied in The Revelation that the destruction of Babylon (not Rome) will happen during the worst earthquake in the history of the world.

"And the seventh angel poured out his vial into the air; and there came a great voice out of the temple of heaven, from the throne, saying, It is done.

18And there were voices, and thunders, and lightnings; and there was a great earthquake, such as was not since men were upon the earth, so mighty an earthquake, and so great.

19And the great city was divided into three parts, and the cities of the nations fell, and great Babylon came in remembrance before God, to give unto her the cup of the wine of the fierceness of his wrath."

Revelation 18:10, 19

Twice in this chapter the Lord promises that **the destruction will take just one hour**. *"Standing afar off for the fear of her torment, saying, Alas, alas, that great city Babylon, that mighty city! for in one hour is thy judgment come."* *And they cast dust on their heads, and cried, weeping and wailing, saying, Alas, alas, that great city, wherein were made rich all that had ships in the sea by reason of her costliness! for in one hour is she made desolate."*

Revelation 18:21

The final destruction of Babylon will be so catastrophic, it is compared to an angel casting a huge bolder into the ocean. *"And a mighty angel took up a stone like a great millstone, and cast it into the sea, saying, Thus with violence shall that great city Babylon be thrown down, and shall be found no more at all."*

Wake up Christians!!

There will be saved people in Babylon right up until this time, probably because of the unbelievable business opportunities, construction jobs, high wages, tax benefits, etc. This is God's last call to anyone who wants to escape the coming holocaust.

Sin Debt

Few people realize how enormous the great "sin debt" that mankind has accumulated. Few people realize that it all began in Babylon.

1. Babylon is the source of all false religion in history and in the world today.

2. Babylon is the source of all evil political systems in history and in the world today. This includes Nimrod, Nebuchadnezzar, Marx, Lenin, Hitler, Stalin, Sadaam Hussein, and eventually the Beast of The Revelation.

3. Babylon is where the worship of mammon (money) began.

4. Babylon is the very place where the Jews went into captivity in 600 BC. They never again worshiped gods of stone, but they came away from Babylon *intoxicated with the love of money* and the ability to make money.

SUMMARY

1. Babylon has never been completely destroyed.

2. Mystery Babylon will play a major role in the latter days

of history.

3. The Arab nations compose only 8% of the world's population; yet they control 75% of the world's oil.

4. In the opinion of this present writer, Babylon, whoever she is (Rome, Babylon itself, or Mecca) will become the center of commerce in government of the Great Tribulation.

5. Babylon will finally be destroyed in the coming Day of The Lord, as these prophecies describe.

CHAPTER 19

THE RETURN OF CHRIST WITH HIS CHURCH

When we began our study of The Revelation we pointed out that Rev. 1:19 reveals the three divisions of the book. *"Write the things which thou hast seen, and the things which are, and the things which shall be hereafter."* The things which *thou has seen* refers to the past. *The things which are* referred to things that were going on in Johns' day. And *the things which shall be hereafter* refer to things that were still future.

The Church Age: Chapters 1-3 refer to the church age up until the Rapture of the church.

The Tribulation: Chapters 4-19 describe events which will occur during the Tribulation. Chapters 19-22 deal with the "Consummation."

The Consummation: When we come to chapter 19 of The Revelation, we come to three of the most important events of the latter days.

- The Second Coming of Jesus Christ
- The Marriage Supper of the Lamb; and
- The Battle of Armageddon.

265

Two of these events, the Second Coming of Christ and the Battle of Armageddon, are familiar to most of us. But for some reason, the Marriage Supper of the Lamb is *seldom mentioned*. How many sermons have you heard on the Marriage Supper of the Lamb? Why is so little said about, what will be the most exciting event in the life of every Christian?

The end of the Tribulation (19:1-6): "*And after these things I heard a great voice of much people in heaven, saying, Alleluia; Salvation, and glory, and honor, and power, unto the Lord our God:*

²For true and righteous are his judgments: for he hath judged the great whore, which did corrupt the earth with her fornication, and hath avenged the blood of his servants at her hand.

³And again they said, Alleluia. And her smoke rose up for ever and ever.

⁴And the four and twenty elders and the four beasts fell down and worshiped God that sat on the throne, saying, Amen; Alleluia.

⁵And a voice came out of the throne, saying, Praise our God, all ye his servants, and ye that fear him, both small and great.

⁶And I heard as it were the voice of a great multitude, and as the voice of many waters, and as the voice of mighty thunderings, saying, Alleluia: for the Lord God omnipotent reigneth."

THE MARRIAGE OF THE LAMB (19: 7-10)

[7]"Let us be glad and rejoice, and give honor to him: for the marriage of the Lamb is come, and his wife hath made herself ready.

[8]And to her was granted that she should be arrayed in fine linen, clean and white: for the fine linen is the righteousness of saints.

*[9]And he saith unto me, Write, Blessed are they which are called unto the **marriage supper** of the Lamb. And he saith unto me, These are the true sayings of God.*

[10]And I fell at his feet to worship him. And he said unto me, See thou do it not: I am thy fellow-servant, and of thy brethren that have the testimony of Jesus: worship God: for the testimony of Jesus is the spirit of prophecy."

The importance of this occasion

We are all familiar with great celebrations down here on earth. There are Oscar Awards, Academy Awards, American Idol, Country Music Awards, Miss America, Miss Universe, and Nobel Peace Prizes, down here on earth. However, these earthly events are less than nothing compare to the glory and majesty of the event known as the Marriage of the Lamb. This event will be the most impressive ceremony ever witnessed by human beings.

EIGHT FACTS ABOUT THIS CREMONY

Here are several basic questions about the Marriage of the Lamb all believers should seriously consider. Who's getting married? Who is this "wife" spoken of in verse 7? Where is this wedding going to take place? When will this wedding take place? Who are the invited guests? Do you plan to attend this wedding? What do you plan to wear to this wedding?

What is the difference between the Marriage of the Lamb and the Marriage Supper of the Lamb? To fully understand what the Marriage of the Lamb is all about, it is important to understand the Jewish wedding customs. The Jewish wedding had three parts: The betrothal, the ceremony, and the celebration. All three of these teach important lessons about the believers' relationship with Jesus Christ.

1. The betrothal (engagement)

A Jewish couple planning to get married would begin with the betrothal (or espousal). The Jewish betrothal was similar to our engagement, but was as binding as marriage itself. As strange as it may seem to our Western minds, this portion of the marriage was often managed by the parents of the couple while the bride and groom were still children. In any case, when a man and a woman would officially become betrothed, this agreement would be as legally and morally binding as marriage itself. There was no physical contact and there was no "dating" other people.

Normally, when adults like Joseph and Mary were betrothed, the couple would go their separate ways for approximately one year and diligently prepare themselves for the wedding itself.

During that period of time between the betrothal and the actual ceremony, the groom would be preparing a home for he and bride to live in. While the groom was building a home for them to live in, the bride would be getting her wardrobe ready. Then, on a date known only to the groom, he and his friends would suddenly appear and escort the bride to the ceremony.

2. The Ceremony

The wedding ceremony would follow and the husband and wife would enjoy a personal, physical relationship for the first time.

3. The Reception

Following the wedding ceremony, there was a reception where the bride and groom with all of their friends would enjoy a great celebration. The marriage of the Lamb will follow the same pattern.

The marriage described in Revelation 19 is the marriage of Jesus Christ, The Lamb of God, and His bride, the church. **The marriage itself will take place in heaven**, following the Rapture, while the earth is going through the Great Tribulation. **The Reception (Supper) will take place on earth,** during the Millennium, when Christ returns to earth with His church.

We are betrothed (engaged) to Christ

The church is composed of individual believers who will become the Bride of Christ. During the present time, referred to as the "Church Age," we believers are "betrothed" (engaged) to Christ. We have known Him and love him by faith, but have not had any physical contact with Christ yet.

(2 Corinthians 11:2): *"For I am jealous over you with godly jealousy: for **I have espoused you** to one husband, that I may present you as a **chaste virgin** to Christ."*

This is the same word used to describe the relationship between Joseph and Mary in (Matthew 1:18-19).

*"Now the birth of Jesus Christ was on this wise: When as his mother Mary was **espoused** to Joseph, before they came together, she was found with child of the Holy Ghost.*

¹⁹Then Joseph her husband, being a just man, and not willing to make her a public example, was minded to put her away privily."

The contract between the believer and Jesus is binding. He expects us to be faithful to Him and not "cheat on Him" while He is "out of town."

(James 4:4) warns us that "dating the world" while you are engaged to Jesus is spiritual adultery. *"Ye adulterers and adulteresses, know ye not that the friendship of the world is enmity with God? whosoever therefore will be a friend of the world is the enemy of God."*

Building a Home

What is Jesus doing now? He is building you a house (John 14:1-30). *"Let not your heart be troubled: ye believe in God, believe also in me. ²In my Father's house are many mansions: if it were not so, I would have told you. I go to prepare a place for you. ³And if I go and prepare a place for you, I will come again, and receive you unto myself; that where I am, there ye may be also."*

Getting Wardrobe Ready

What should we be doing now? While we are waiting for Christ to return, serious believers should be getting their wardrobes ready.

Our wedding clothes (Rev. 19:7-8)

Do you realize what we are going to wear to this marriage of Christ and His Church? Verse 8, literally translated says: *"The fine linen is the righteous acts of the saints."*

7"Let us be glad and rejoice, and give honor to him: for the marriage of the Lamb is come, and his wife hath made herself ready.

8And to her was granted that she should be arrayed in fine linen, clean and white: for the fine linen is the righteousness of saints."

Saved by Grace but dressed in our works

This might seem strange to some, but the Bible teaches clear that we are saved entirely by Grace through Faith. But our works (after salvation) will make up the clothes we will wear to this wedding. This is important! Our good works have nothing at all to do with our salvation, but they have everything to do with our future rewards and our wedding garments.

The ceremony and the reception

The Marriage and the Marriage Supper will take place at different times and in different places. In our opinion, believers will go immediately to heaven at the Rapture (Revelation 4:1) and the actual marriage ceremony between Christ and the church will take place in heaven at that time. When we come back with Christ in Revelation 19, we will celebrate the "Supper" or the "Wedding Reception." Also, the participants of these two events will be different.

Dwight Pentecost

Consider what Dwight Pentecost said concerning the wedding and the supper.

1. "It seems necessary to distinguish between the Marriage of the Lamb and the Marriage Supper."

2. "The Marriage is an event that has particular reference to the church and takes place in heaven."

3. "The Marriage Supper is an event that involves Israel and takes place on the earth."

4. "In Matthew 22:1-14, Luke 14:16-24, and Matthew 15:1-13, where Israel is waiting the return of the Bridegroom and the Bride, the wedding feast or supper is located on earth and has particular reference to Israel."

5. "The wedding supper, then, becomes the parabolic picture of the entire Millennium age, to which Israel will be invited during the Tribulation period, which invitation many will reject and so they will be cast out, and many will accept the invitation and will be received in."

6. "Because of the rejection, the invitation will likewise go to the Gentiles so that many of them will be included."

7. "Israel, at the Second Advent, will be waiting for the Bridegroom to come from the wedding ceremony and invite them to the Supper, at which time the Bridegroom will introduce His bride to His friends."

(Matthew 25:1-13): "*Then the kingdom of heaven shall be likened to ten virgins who took their lamps and went out to meet the bridegroom.*

2 Now five of them were wise, and five were foolish. 3 Those who were foolish took their lamps and took no oil with them, 4 but the wise took oil in their vessels with their lamps.

5. While the bridegroom was delayed, they all slumbered and slept. 6 And at midnight a cry was heard: 'Behold, the bridegroom is coming; go out to meet him!'

7 Then all those virgins arose and trimmed their lamps. And the foolish said to the wise, 'Give us some of your oil, for our lamps are going out.'

9 But the wise answered, saying, 'No, lest there should not be enough for us and you; but go rather to those who sell, and buy for yourselves.'

10 And while they went to buy, the bridegroom came, and those who were ready went in with him to the wedding; and the door was shut. 11 Afterward the other virgins came also, saying, 'Lord, Lord, open to us!' 12 But he answered and said, 'Assuredly, I say to you, I do not know you.'

13 Watch therefore, for you know neither the day nor the hour in which the Son of Man is coming."

The participants at the supper (Luke 14:16-24)

16 "Then He said to him, "A certain man gave a great supper and invited many,   17 and sent his servant at supper time to say to those who were invited, 'Come, for all things are now ready.'

18 But they all with one accord began to make excuses. The first said to him, 'I have bought a piece of ground, and I must go and see it. I ask you to have me excused.'

19 And another said, 'I have bought five yoke of oxen, and I am going to test them. I ask you to have me excused.'

20 Still another said, 'I have married a wife, and therefore I cannot come.' 21 So that servant came and reported these things to his master.

Then the master of the house, being angry, said to his servant, 'Go out quickly into the streets and lanes of the city, and bring in here the poor and the maimed and the lame and the blind.'

22 And the servant said, 'Master, it is done as you commanded, and still there is room.'

23 Then the master said to the servant, 'Go out into the highways and hedges, and compel them to come in, that my house may be filled. 24 For I say to you that none of those men who were invited shall taste my supper.' "

WHO ARE THE INVITED GUESTS?

Christ and the church will attend the actually marriage ceremony.

Invited guests will attend the reception (supper). Here is a list of those we believe will be invited to celebrate the reception with us.

1. All of the saints of the Old Testament will be invited.

2. The 144,000 Jews who were sealed during the Tribulation will be there.

3. The Tribulation Martyrs will all be there.

4. The Two Witnesses will be there.

5. The Angel who preached the Everlasting Gospel will also attend.

6. The saved out of Israel who turned to Christ when their blindness was removed (Romans 11) will be guests.

(Romans 11:25-29): *25 "For I do not desire, brethren, that you should be ignorant of this mystery, lest you should be wise in your own opinion, that blindness in part has happened to Israel until the fullness of the Gentiles has come in.*

26 And so all Israel will be saved, as it is written: "The Deliverer will come out of Zion, And He will turn away ungodliness from

Jacob;

27 For this is My covenant with them, When I take away their sins."

28 Concerning the gospel they are enemies for your sake, but concerning the election they are beloved for the sake of the fathers.

29 For the gifts and the calling of God are irrevocable."

PRACTICAL APPLICATION

1. God expects good works from every person who is really saved (Ephesians 2:10)

"For we are his workmanship, created in Christ Jesus unto good works, which God hath before ordained that we should walk in them."

2. True Salvation always produces good works. If there are no good works there is probably no salvation (James 2:14-26).

14. "What does it profit, my brethren, if someone says he has faith but does not have works? Can faith save him?

15. If a brother or sister is naked and destitute of daily food,

16. and one of you says to them, "Depart in peace, be warmed and filled," but you do not give them the things which are needed for the body, what does it profit?

17. Thus also faith by itself, if it does not have works, is dead.

18. But someone will say, "You have faith, and I have works." Show me your faith without your works, and I will show you my faith by my works.

19.   You believe that there is one God. You do well. Even the demons believe--and tremble!

20. But do you want to know, O foolish man, that faith without works is dead?

21. Was not Abraham our father justified by works when he offered Isaac his son on the altar?

22. Do you see that faith was working together with his works, and by works faith was made perfect?

23. And the Scripture was fulfilled which says, "Abraham believed God, and it was accounted to him for righteousness." And he was called the friend of God.

24. You see then that a man is **justified by works***, and not by faith only.*

25. Likewise, was not **Rahab the harlot also justified by works** *when she received the messengers and sent them out another way?*

26. For as the body without the spirit is dead, so **faith without works is dead** *also.*

3. The clothes you will wear to the wedding (wedding dress) are being made up from the good works you perform in the Name of Jesus Christ.

When the Bible says in Revelation 19:7 that the bride (that's us) has "made herself ready, "this means that we are busy working and doing something for Jesus.

4. Not only are we expected to do good works for Jesus, we will also be judged and rewarded for our works (2 Cor. 5:10):

"For we must all appear before the judgment seat of Christ, that each one may receive the things done in the body, according to what he has done, whether good or bad."

There are two kinds of works (1 Cor. 3:10-15)

10 *"According to the grace of God which was given to me, as a wise master builder I have laid the foundation, and another builds on it. But let each one take heed how he builds on it.*

11. For no other foundation can anyone lay than that which is laid, which is Jesus Christ. 12. Now if anyone builds on this foundation with gold, silver, precious stones, wood, hay, straw,

13. each one's work will become clear; for the Day will declare it, because it will be revealed by fire; and the fire will test each one's work, of what sort it is.14. If anyone's work which he has built on it endures, he will receive a reward. 15. If anyone's work is burned, he will suffer loss; but he himself will be saved, yet so as through fire. **Will you be there? What do you plan to wear?**

THE BATTLE OF ARMAGEDDON

There are three major battles foretold in prophecy and it is easy to get them confused.

- God and Magog (Ezekiel 38-39);

- Armageddon (Rev. 14:14-20), (Rev. 16:14-16), & (Rev. 19:11-21); 3)

- The Final Rebellion (Rev. 20:7-10).

The battle of Gog and Magog could *possibly* be fought toward the end of the church age, which means this battle could take place in our lifetime. Armageddon will be fought at the end of the Tribulation. The final rebellion will be fought at the end of the Millennium. The focus of this study will be the Battle of Armageddon. But first, let's review.

A QUICK REVIEW

In our study of chapters 4-19, we've been dealing with things which will take place during the Tribulation. Chapter 6 gives us a summary of the entire Tribulation period. When we come to the last part of chapter 19, The Tribulation is over and the Kingdom is about to begin. Here is a brief outline of what we've studied up until this point.

1. The Church Age (Rev. 2-3)

Chapters 2-3 deal with the church age from the Day of Pentecost until Christ comes for His church at the Rapture.

2. The Rapture (Rev. 4:1)

Christ will return for His church at the end of the present Church Age. The Tribulation cannot begin as long as the church is in the world.

(2 Thess. 2:3-7): *"Let no man deceive you by any means: for that day shall not come, except there come a falling away first, and that man of sin be revealed, the son of perdition;*

4 Who opposeth and exalteth himself above all that is called God, or that is worshiped; so that he as God sitteth in the temple of God, showing himself that he is God.

5 Remember ye not, that, when I was yet with you, I told you these things?

6 And now ye know what withholdeth that he might be revealed in his time.

7 For the mystery of iniquity doth already work: only he who now letteth will let, until he be taken out of the way.

3. The Tribulation (Revelation, chapters 4-19)

(2 Thess. 2:8-12) *8And then shall that Wicked be revealed, whom the Lord shall consume with the spirit of his mouth, and shall destroy with the brightness of his coming: 9 Even him, whose coming is after the working of Satan with all power and signs and lying wonders,*

10 And with all deceivableness of unrighteousness in them that perish; because they received not the love of the truth, that they might be saved.

11And for this cause God shall send them strong delusion, that they should believe a lie:

12 That they all might be damned who believed not the truth, but had pleasure in unrighteousness. "

4. The False Messiah: As soon as the church is gone, the rider on the white horse will appear (Rev. 6:2). This is a "false Christ." This man may well be the "Mahdi" the Muslims are looking for.

A gifted leader

This man will be extremely "gifted" and a master of diplomacy. *The reason he will be so persuasive is because he is literally indwelt by Satan.*

A ten nation federation

This false Christ will gain control of the ten nation federation (Could this possibly be the European Union?).

Brief Peace

This man will be hailed as the greatest peace-maker in history and one of his major accomplishments will be to bring about a peace treaty between Israel and her enemies.

(Daniel 9:27): *"And he shall confirm the covenant with many for one week: and in the midst of the week he shall cause the sacrifice and the oblation to cease, and for the overspreading of abominations he shall make it desolate, even until the consummation, and that determined shall be poured upon the desolate."*

We believe this will happen during the first part of the

Tribulation.

Israel will be allowed to occupy her land for a brief period. This False Messiah will arrange this peace.

The Jewish temple will be rebuilt on the Temple Mount and sacrifices will be reinstated as in the Old Testament.[118]

He will break the peace Treaty

In the middle of the "week" (3½ years into the 7 year Tribulation), something will happen. This false Messiah will "take off his disguise" and his true nature will become known. He will bring an end to the peace treaty. Sacrifices will be stopped. The temple will be desecrated.

"The Man of Sin" will demand worship (2 Thess. 2:3-5)

"Let no man deceive you by any means: for that day shall not come, except there come a falling away first, and that man of sin be revealed, the son of perdition;

4 Who opposeth and exalteth himself above all that is called God, or that is worshipped; so that he as God sitteth in the temple of God, showing himself that he is God.

5 Remember ye not, that, when I was yet with you, I told you these things?"

Abomination of Desolation

The Tribulation is a period of seven years. The first half of this period is a time of peace. The last half is a time of suffering. We call the last half of the Tribulation the

---

[118]Preparations are being made for this at this very moment. Joel Rosenberg has some interesting information about this. Read his book, **Epicenter,** for a starter.

"Great" Tribulation. Jesus warned of those days. He warned the people who would be living in Israel at that time to "flee to the mountains."

(Matt. 24:15-22): *"When ye therefore shall see the abomination of desolation, spoken of by Daniel the prophet, stand in the holy place, (whoso readeth, let him understand.)*

16Then let them which be in Judaea flee into the mountains:

17Let him which is on the housetop not come down to take any thing out of his house:

18Neither let him which is in the field return back to take his clothes.

19And woe unto them that are with child, and to them that give suck in those days!

20But pray ye that your flight be not in the winter, neither on the Sabbath day:

21For then shall be great tribulation, such as was not since the beginning of the world to this time, no, nor ever shall be.

22And except those days should be shortened, there should no flesh be saved: but for the elect's sake those days shall be shortened."

The Battle of Armageddon itself

This is the "Second Coming of Christ," called the Revelation. His coming *for* His church in (Rev. 4:1) is called the "Rapture." His coming *with* His church in this chapter is called the Revelation.

11 And I saw heaven opened, and behold a white horse; and he that sat upon him was called Faithful and True, and in righteousness he doth judge and make war.

[12]His eyes were as a flame of fire, and on his head were many crowns; and he had a name written, that no man knew, but he himself.

[13]And he was clothed with a vesture dipped in blood: and his name is called The Word of God.

[14]And the armies which were in heaven followed him upon white horses, clothed in fine linen, white and clean.

[15]And out of his mouth goeth a sharp sword, that with it he should smite the nations: and he shall rule them with a rod of iron: and he treadeth the winepress of the fierceness and wrath of Almighty God.

[16]And he hath on his vesture and on his thigh a name written, KING OF KINGS, AND LORD OF LORDS.

[17]And I saw an angel standing in the sun; and he cried with a loud voice, saying to all the fowls that fly in the midst of heaven, Come and gather yourselves together unto the supper of the great God;

[18]That ye may eat the flesh of kings, and the flesh of captains, and the flesh of mighty men, and the flesh of horses, and of them that sit on them, and the flesh of all men, both free and bond, both small and great.

(Rev. 19:19-21) *[19]And I saw the beast, and the kings of the earth, and their armies, gathered together to make war against him that sat on the horse, and against his army.*

[20]And the beast was taken, and with him the false prophet that wrought miracles before him, with which he deceived them that had received the mark of the beast, and them that worshiped his image. These both were cast alive into a lake of fire burning with

brimstone.

²¹And the remnant were slain with the sword of him that sat upon the horse, which sword proceeded out of his mouth: and all the fowls were filled with their flesh."

Everything will change

The Battle of Armageddon will bring about some drastic changes in the way God deals with sinful men.

1. No More Mercy

This battle marks the end of God's efforts to save men. From Genesis to Revelation God is seen "striving" to save men from their sins. Just before the flood, God warned that His Spirit will not always strive with men," yet God gave Noah's generation 120 more years to repent before He sent the flood. At this point in history (Revelation 19), God stops trying. From this point on, it's all over! From this point on, sinners receive what they so richly deserve.

2. No More Choices

From the very beginning of history, God has given men the freedom to make certain choices. God would allow men to choose to believe in God or they could choose to become Atheists; Men could choose to repent of their sins and escape the wrath of God, or they could continue in their sins and receive Divine retribution. When we reach this point in history, man no longer has any options! Everything is completely out of his control. He is going to be judged, punished, and damned and there is nothing he can do to escape it. At this point, it's even too late to pray!!

3. No More Human Government

This battle marks the end of every form of human government. There will be no more Monarchy, Anarchy, Communism, Socialism, or even Democracy. From this point on, Christ will "smite the nations and rule with a rod of iron." Man has had his "day." Now, it's God's turn!

4. The End of Times of the Gentiles

This will also mark the end of a period Jesus called "The times of the Gentiles."

(Luke 21:24-27): *"And they shall fall by the edge of the sword, and shall be led away captive into all nations: and Jerusalem shall be trodden down of the Gentiles, until the times of the Gentiles be fulfilled.*

25And there shall be signs in the sun, and in the moon, and in the stars; and upon the earth distress of nations, with perplexity; the sea and the waves roaring;

26Men's hearts failing them for fear, and for looking after those things which are coming on the earth: for the powers of heaven shall be shaken.

27And then shall they see the Son of man coming in a cloud with power and great glory."

THIS BATTLE WILL INVOLVE ALL NATIONS

1. Evil Spirits Entice Nations (Rev. 16:13-14)

"And I saw three unclean spirits like frogs come out of the mouth of the dragon, and out of the mouth of the beast, and out of the mouth of the false prophet.

*14For they are the spirits of devils, working miracles, which go forth unto the **kings of the earth and of the whole world**, to*

287

gather them to the battle of that great day of God Almighty."

2. Specific Nations Mentioned (Daniel 11). This battle will involve all nations. However, Daniel mentions certain nations specifically.

- The Beast and his Kingdom (Daniel 11: 36-37)

- The King of the South (Daniel 11:40)

- Israel, called the "Glorious Land." (Daniel 11:41)

- Edom Moab, and Ammon (Daniel 11:41)

- Egypt, Lybia, and Ethiopia (Daniel 11:42)

- China (Daniel 11:44) "Tidings from the East."

- *What's left* of Russia (Daniel 11:44) "Tidings from the North."

3. Specific Geographical Areas Mentioned

This battle will be fought over a 200 mile area, but will be concentrated around Jerusalem, but specific nations are mentioned in prophecy.

- Jerusalem is mentioned (Zechariah 12:1-2)

- Edom is mentioned (Isa. 34:5) (63:1-6)

- The Valley of Jehosaphat (Joel 3:2,12)

- Megiddo (Armageddon) (Rev. 16:16)

The beast cast into lake of fire (Rev. 10:20)

And the beast was taken, and with him the false prophet that wrought miracles before him, with which he deceived them that had received the mark of the beast, and them that worshiped his image. These both were cast alive into a lake of fire burning with brimstone.

A feast for the buzzards (Rev. 19:21)

²¹And the remnant were slain with the sword of him that sat upon the horse, which sword proceeded out of his mouth: and all the fowls were filled with their flesh."

THE RESULTS OF THIS BATTLE

1. Israel's Blindness Lifted

For years, for reasons known only to God, there has been a veil of spiritual blindness on Israel.[119] At this point, when the armies surround Jerusalem and God intervenes, the prophecies of Zechariah will be fulfilled.

(Zechariah 10:8-14): *8. In that day the Lord will defend the inhabitants of Jerusalem; the one who is feeble among them in that day shall be like David, and the house of David shall be like God, like the Angel of the Lord before them.*

9. It shall be in that day that I will seek to destroy all the nations that come against Jerusalem.

10. "And I will pour on the house of David and on the inhabitants of Jerusalem the Spirit of grace and supplication; then they will look on Me whom they pierced. Yes, they will mourn for Him as one mourns for his only son, and grieve for Him as one grieves for a firstborn.

11. In that day there shall be a great mourning in Jerusalem, like the mourning at Hadad Rimmon in the plain of Megiddo.

---

[119]Read Romans 11 at the end of this lesson.

12. And the land shall mourn, every family by itself: the family of the house of David by itself, and their wives by themselves; the family of the house of Nathan by itself, and their wives by themselves;

13. the family of the house of Levi by itself, and their wives by themselves; the family of Shimei by itself, and their wives by themselves;

14. All the families that remain, every family by itself, and their wives by themselves. (The New King James Version)

2. Israel will have been Refined and Purified and be ready for Jesus (Zechariah 13:8-9)

8. And it shall come to pass in all the land," Says the Lord, "That two-thirds in it shall be cut off and die, But one-third shall be left in it:

9. I will bring the one-third through the fire, Will refine them as silver is refined, and test them as gold is tested. They will call on My name, And I will answer them. I will say, 'This is My people'; And each one will say, 'The Lord is my God."

3. Jesus will return and stand on the Mount of Olives (Zechariah 14:2-9)

2. For I will gather all the nations to battle against Jerusalem; The city shall be taken, The houses rifled, And the women ravished. Half of the city shall go into captivity, But the remnant of the people shall not be cut off from the city.

3. Then the Lord will go forth and fight against those nations, As He fights in the day of battle.

4. And in that day His feet will stand on the Mount of Olives, Which faces Jerusalem on the east. And the Mount of Olives shall be split in two, From east to west, Making a very large valley; Half of the mountain shall move toward the north And half of it toward the south.

5. Then you shall flee through My mountain valley, For the mountain valley shall reach to Azal. Yes, you shall flee As you fled from the earthquake In the days of Uzziah king of Judah. Thus the Lord my God will come, And all the saints with You.

6. It shall come to pass in that day there will be no light; the lights will diminish.

7. It shall be one day which is known to the Lord-- neither day nor night. But at evening time it shall happen that it will be light.

8. And in that day it shall be that living waters shall flow from Jerusalem, half of them toward the eastern sea And half of them toward the western sea; In both summer and winter it shall occur.

9. And the Lord shall be King over all the earth. In that day it shall be-- "The Lord is one," And His name one."

Israel will be restored (Romans 11)

1 I say then, Hath God cast away his people? God forbid. For I also am an Israelite, of the seed of Abraham, of the tribe of Benjamin.

2 God hath not cast away his people which he foreknew. wot ye not what the scripture saith of Elias? How he maketh intercession to God against Israel, saying,

3 Lord, they have killed thy prophets, and digged down thine altars; and I am left alone, and they seek my life.

4 But what saith the answer of God unto him? I have reserved to myself seven thousand men, who have not bowed the knee to the image of Baal.

5 Even so then at this present time also there is a remnant according to the election of grace.

6 And if by grace, then is it no more of works: otherwise grace is no more grace. But if it be of works, then is it no more grace: otherwise work is no more work.

7 What then? Israel hath not obtained that which he seeketh for; but the election hath obtained it, and the rest were blinded

8 (According as it is written, God hath given them the spirit of slumber, eyes that they should not see, and ears that they should not hear;) unto this day.

9 And David saith, Let their table be made a snare, and a trap, and a stumbling-block, and a recompence unto them:

10 Let their eyes be darkened, that they may not see, and bow down their back always.

11 I say then, Have they stumbled that they should fall? God forbid: but rather through their fall salvation is come unto the Gentiles, for to provoke them to jealousy.

12 Now if the fall of them be the riches of the world, and the diminishing of them the riches of the Gentiles; how much more their fulness?

13 For I speak to you Gentiles, inasmuch as I am the apostle of the Gentiles, I magnify mine office:

14 If by any means I may provoke to emulation them which are my flesh, and might save some of them.

15 For if the casting away of them be the reconciling of the world, what shall the receiving of them be, but life from the dead?

16 For if the firstfruit be holy, the lump is also holy: and if the root be holy, so are the branches.

17 And if some of the branches be broken off, and thou, being a wild olive tree, wert graffed in among them, and with them partakest of the root and fatness of the olive tree;

18 Boast not against the branches. But if thou boast, thou bearest not the root, but the root thee.

19 Thou wilt say then, The branches were broken off, that I might be graffed in.

20 Well; because of unbelief they were broken off, and thou standest by faith. Be not high-minded, but fear:

21 For if God spared not the natural branches, take heed lest he also spare not thee.

22 Behold therefore the goodness and severity of God: on them which fell, severity; but toward thee, goodness, if thou continue in his goodness: otherwise thou also shalt be cut off.

23 And they also, if they abide not still in unbelief, shall be graffed in: for God is able to graff them in again.

24 For if thou wert cut out of the olive tree which is wild by nature, and wert graffed contrary to nature into a good olive tree: how much more shall these, which be the natural branches, be graffed into their own olive tree?

25 For I would not, brethren, that ye should be ignorant of this mystery, lest ye should be wise in your own conceits; that blindness in part is happened to Israel, until the fulness of the Gentiles be come in.

26 And so all Israel shall be saved: as it is written, There shall come out of Zion the Deliverer, and shall turn away ungodliness from Jacob:

27 For this is my covenant unto them, when I shall take away their sins.

28 As concerning the gospel, they are enemies for your sakes: but as touching the election, they are beloved for the fathers' sakes.

29 For the gifts and calling of God are without repentance.

30 For as ye in times past have not believed God, yet have now obtained mercy through their unbelief:

31 Even so have these also now not believed, that through your mercy they also may obtain mercy.

32 For God hath concluded them all in unbelief, that he might have mercy upon all.

33 O the depth of the riches both of the wisdom and knowledge of God! how unsearchable are his judgments, and his ways past finding out!

34 For who hath known the mind of the Lord? or who hath been his counselor?

35 Or who hath first given to him, and it shall be recompensed unto him again?

36 For of him, and through him, and to him, are all things: to whom be glory forever. Amen.

CHAPTER 20

PEACE ON EARTH

When we come to chapter 20 of The Revelation we have come to what we may call "The Last Chapter of World History." In this chapter we read about end of a number of things:

1. The end of all forms of human government.

2. The end of Satan and his work on earth.

3. The end of all sin and rebellion against God.

4. The end of all wars.

5. The end of death and hell.

SATAN BOUND

The first thing we will read about is the binding of Satan. In this chapter Satan is cast into the abyss, and for the first time since Adam, there will be peace on earth (Rev. 20:1-3).

"And I saw an angel come down from heaven, having the key of the bottomless pit and a great chain in his hand.

2And he laid hold on the dragon, that old serpent, which is the

Devil, and Satan, and bound him a thousand years,

3And cast him into the bottomless pit, and shut him up, and set a seal upon him, that he should deceive the nations no more, till the thousand years should be fulfilled: and after that he must be loosed a little season."

- Some Bible scholars teach that the binding of Satan took place during the "inter-advent" period (the time between Christ's first and second coming).

- If they are correct, and Satan is already bound, then who's been doing His work for the last 2000 years?

- If they are correct, how could Satan enter Judas, tempt Peter, blind unbelievers (2 Cor. 4:4), and cause you and me such grief?

- Other scholars teach that chapter refers to the *intermediate state* between the time a believer dies and he/she is resurrected.

- The Roman Catholic Church follows St. Augustine, who rejected the idea of a literal Millennium taught that chapter 20 refers to this present age. They also believe the Kingdom is the church. ***God help us!!!***

CHRIST WILL ESTABLISH HIS KINGDOM

When we come to chapter 20, we come to the most controversial chapter in the entire book of The Revelation.

The major controversy revolves around this period of one thousand years that is mentioned six times in seven verses.

The way a person interprets the 1000 years determines whether that person is a Pre-millennialist, a Post-millennialist, or an A-millennialist.

THREE VIEWS OF THE KINGDOM

The Kingdom is Literal

The prophecies regarding the Kingdom of Christ were given to be taken literally. Israel is Israel and the church is the church. God has a plan for both Israel and the church in the latter days. A literal Jesus will return to a literal earth; When He returns He will set up an earthly kingdom and will reign over all the earth, from the Throne of David, for a literal period of one-thousand years.

The Kingdom is Not Literal

The Old Testament prophecies about the kingdom, plus the references in The Revelation are *"allegorical."* *This means they are not supposed to be taken literally.* This theory was introduced by a man named Origen in Alexandria.

The Kingdom is the Church

This was the position of St. Augustine presented in his monumental work, "The City of God." This is the Roman

Catholic position. They believed that the church is the Kingdom and the Pope is the Vicar of Christ on earth.

Note: Many non-Catholics have also adopted a modified view of this. They reject the idea that the Roman Catholic Church is the Kingdom, but they reason something like this:

- The prophecies of the Kingdom were first given for Israel;

- But since the Jews rejected Jesus, those prophecies are *now cancelled or have been applied to the church.*

- In other words, God has no plan for the Jews or Israel today.

- They believe the church is the "Spiritual Israel."

This is a very popular view, but in the opinion of this writer, it is not at all consistent with the Word of God. As far as we can determine, all of the Old Testament prophets, all of the Apostles, and all of the early church leaders believed in a literal, earthly kingdom over which the Messiah would reign.

As far as we know, the idea of a "spiritual" kingdom did not appear until the third century. All of the reputable church leaders until the third century interpreted the Bible literally and believed in a literal kingdom.

It was not until the third century after Christ that people began to follow the teachings of a man named Origen, and later St. Augustine, the Roman Catholic Theologian, and began to "spiritualize" the clear teachings of the Word of God.

For the first 200 years of church history, the early church clearly believed in the Pre-millennial return of Christ and a literal one-thousand year period of peace on earth.

It was not until the time of a man named Origen, and later, the Catholic Theologian named Augustine, that men began to *spiritualize* the Scriptures and reject the idea of a literal kingdom on earth.

The Form of Government (Rev. 20:4-6)

The second thing we see in chapter 20 is the form of government that will be in operation during the Millennium (Rev. 20:4-6). A literal Jesus Christ will reign on a literal earth for a literal 1000 years.

4And I saw thrones, and they sat upon them, and judgment was given unto them: and I saw the souls of them that were beheaded for the witness of Jesus, and for the word of God, and which had not worshiped the beast, neither his image, neither had received his mark upon their foreheads, or in their hands; and they lived and reigned with Christ a thousand years.

5 But the rest of the dead lived not again until the thousand years were finished. This is the first resurrection.

6Blessed and holy is he that hath part in the first resurrection: on such the second death hath no power, but they shall be priests of God and of Christ, and shall reign with him a thousand years."

This will fulfill the promise of Jesus to His disciples in Matthew 19:27-28. *"Then Peter answered and said to Him, "See, we have left all and followed You. Therefore what shall we have?" So Jesus said to them, "Assuredly I say to you, that in the regeneration, when the Son of Man sits on the throne of His glory, you who have followed Me will also sit on twelve thrones,*

299

judging the twelve tribes of Israel."

This will fulfill the promise of Jesus to the saints of the church are in 1 Corinthians 6:2. *"Do you not know that the saints will judge the world? And if the world will be judged by you, are you unworthy to judge the smallest matters?"*

This will fulfill the promise of God to the martyrs in Revelation 20:4. *"And I saw thrones, and they sat on them, and judgment was committed to them. Then I saw the souls of those who had been beheaded for their witness to Jesus and for the word of God, who had not worshiped the beast or his image, and had not received his mark on their foreheads or on their hands. And they lived and reigned with Christ for a thousand years."*

Who will be judged by those seated on the thrones?

- Jesus will sit on David's throne and reign over all the earth (2 Samuel 7:12-16) (Jeremiah 30:9) (Ezekiel 37:24-28).

- The Apostles will sit on thrones and judge the 12 Tribes of Israel (Matthew 19:27-28).

- The Saints will judge the world and the angels (1 Corinthians 6:2).

- The Tribulation Martyrs will enjoy a special position as Priests of God.

- The nations will be judged.

- Old Testament Saints will be judged.

- Tribulation Martyrs will be judged.

- Israel will be judged.

- Angels will be judged.

- The world will be judged.

WHAT WILL LIFE BE LIKE IN THE KINGDOM?

1. Satan will be bound for 1000 years (Rev. 20:1-3).

"And I saw an angel come down from heaven, having the key of the bottomless pit and a great chain in his hand.

2And he laid hold on the dragon, that old serpent, which is the Devil, and Satan, and bound him a thousand years,

3And cast him into the bottomless pit, and shut him up, and set a seal upon him, that he should deceive the nations no more, till the thousand years should be fulfilled: and after that he must be loosed a little season."

2. The Saints will reign for 1000 years (Revelation 20:4-6).

4 And I saw thrones, and they sat upon them, and judgment was given unto them: and I saw the souls of them that were beheaded for the witness of Jesus, and for the word of God, and which had not worshipped the beast, neither his image, neither had received his mark upon their foreheads, or in their hands; and they lived and reigned with Christ a thousand years.

5 But the rest of the dead lived not again until the thousand years were finished. This is the first resurrection.

6 Blessed and holy is he that hath part in the first resurrection: on such the second death hath no power, but they shall be priests of God and of Christ, and shall reign with him a thousand years.

301

3. Wild animals will be tame (Isaiah 11:6-9).

6The wolf also shall dwell with the lamb, and the leopard shall lie down with the kid; and the calf and the young lion and the fatling together; and a little child shall lead them.

7And the cow and the bear shall feed; their young ones shall lie down together: and the lion shall eat straw like the ox.

8And the sucking child shall play on the hole of the asp, and the weaned child shall put his hand on the cockatrice' den.

9They shall not hurt nor destroy in all my holy mountain: for the earth shall be full of the knowledge of the LORD, as the waters cover the sea."

4. The Saints will judge the world (I Cor. 6:1-3).

1"Dare any of you, having a matter against another, go to law before the unjust, and not before the saints?

2Do ye not know that the saints shall judge the world? and if the world shall be judged by you, are ye unworthy to judge the smallest matters? Know ye not that we shall judge angels? how much more things that pertain to this life?

5. All wars will end (Isaiah 2:2-4)

2And it shall come to pass in the last days, that the mountain of the LORD'S house shall be established in the top of the mountains, and shall be exalted above the hills; and all nations shall flow unto it.

3And many people shall go and say, Come ye, and let us go up to the mountain of the LORD, to the house of the God of Jacob; and he will teach us of his ways, and we will walk in his paths: for out of Zion shall go forth the law, and the word of the LORD from Jerusalem.

4And He shall judge among the nations, and shall rebuke many people: and they shall beat their swords into plowshares, and their spears into pruning-hooks: nation shall not lift up sword against nation, neither shall they learn war anymore."

6. Jesus will be King over all the earth (Zechariah 14:8-9).

8 "And it shall be in that day, that living waters shall go out from Jerusalem; half of them toward the former sea, and half of them toward the hinder sea: in summer and in winter shall it be. 9 And the LORD shall be king over all the earth: In that day shall there be one LORD."

7. There will be perfect peace (Psalm 72:12-13). There will be perfect peace because, for the first time in history, there will be a perfect government. There will be no innocent people in jail and no guilty people walking the streets. For the first time in history there will be safe streets. *For he shall deliver the needy when he crieth; the poor also, and him that hath no helper. He shall spare the poor and needy, and shall save the souls of the needy,*

8. There will be a perfect environment (Rom. 8:18-23)

There has never been a time so far, when the world has had a chance to see the full potential of God, Man, animal life, vegetable life, and the environment, all living in perfect harmony under the supervision of God. During the millennium, man will have a chance to see what life would have been like on earth if sin had not entered and corrupted Gods' creation. The earth will finally be in balance and the curse will be removed from the earth.

(Romans 8:18-23) *18. "Yet what we suffer now is nothing compared to the glory he will give us after. 19. For all creation is* *waiting eagerly for that future day when God will reveal who his children really are.*

20. Against its will, everything on earth was subjected to God's curse.

21. All creation anticipates the day when it will join God's children in glorious freedom from death and decay.

22. For we know that all creation has been groaning as in the pains of childbirth right up to the present time.

23. And even we Christians, although we have the Holy Spirit within us as a foretaste of future glory, also groan to be released from pain and suffering. We, too, wait anxiously for that day when God will give us our full rights as his children, including the new bodies he has promised us."

9. Perfect Health Care (Isaiah 35:5-6).

For the first and only time in history, we won't need health care or medicine because there won't be much sickness.

5 Then the eyes of the blind shall be opened, and the ears of the deaf shall be unstopped.

6 Then shall the lame man leap as an hart, and the tongue of the dumb sing: for in the wilderness shall waters break out, and streams in the desert."

10. People will live longer (Isaiah 65:20).

"There shall be no more thence an infant of days, nor an old man that hath not filled his days: for the child shall die an hundred years old; but the sinner being an hundred years old shall be accursed."

11. God will open the blind eyes of the Jews. Those who survive the Tribulation will turn to Christ (Zechariah 12:7-10).

"And it shall come to pass in that day, that I will seek to destroy all the nations that come against Jerusalem. 10 And I will pour upon the house of David, and upon the inhabitants of Jerusalem, the spirit of grace and of supplications: and they shall look upon me whom they have pierced, and they shall mourn for him, as one mourneth for his only son, and shall be in bitterness for him, as one that is in bitterness for his firstborn."

(Romans 11:26-29) *"For I would not, brethren, that ye should be ignorant of this mystery, lest ye should be wise in your own conceits; that blindness in part is happened to Israel, until the fulness of the Gentiles be come in.*

26***And so all Israel shall be saved:*** *as it is written, There shall come out of Sion the Deliverer, and shall turn away ungodliness from Jacob:*

27*For this is my covenant unto them, when I shall take away their sins.* 28*As concerning the gospel, they are enemies for your sakes: but as touching the election, they are beloved for the fathers' sakes.*

29*For the gifts and calling of God are without repentance."*

WHO WILL LIVE IN THIS KINGDOM?

Those who take the Bible literally believe that there will be at least five different groups of people alive on earth during Millennial Kingdom.

1. The Resurrected Saints of the New Testament.

2. The Resurrected Saints of the Old Testament.

3. One Third of the Jews in Israel who survive the Great Tribulation (Zech. 13:8-9).

"And it shall come to pass, that in all the land, saith the LORD, two parts therein shall be cut off and die; but the third shall be left therein. And I will bring the third part through the fire, and will refine them as silver is refined, and will try them as gold is tried: they shall call on my name, and I will hear them: I will say, It is my people: and they shall say, The LORD is my God."

4. The Tribulation Martyrs (Rev. 20:4).

"And I saw thrones, and they sat upon them, and judgment was given unto them: and I saw the souls of them that were beheaded for the witness of Jesus, and for the word of God, and which had not worshiped the beast, neither his image, neither had received his mark upon their foreheads, or in their hands; and they lived and reigned with Christ a thousand years."

5. The Tribulation Survivors (Matthew 24:15-22).

15 "When ye therefore shall see the abomination of desolation, spoken of by Daniel the prophet, stand in the holy place, (whoso readeth, let him understand:)

16Then let them which be in Judaea flee into the mountains:

17Let him which is on the housetop not come down to take anything out of his house:

18Neither let him which is in the field return back to take his clothes. 19And woe unto them that are with child, and to them that give suck in those days!

20But pray ye that your flight be not in the winter, neither on the Sabbath day:

21For then shall be great tribulation, such as was not since the beginning of the world to this time, no, nor ever shall be.

22And except those days should be shortened, there should no flesh be saved: but for the elect's sake those days shall be shortened."

WHEN WILL CHRIST ESTABLISH HIS KINGDOM?

There are those who teach that Christ returned in AD 70, Satan is bound, and we are now in the Kingdom. They argue that the Kingdom of heaven is the reign of Jesus Christ in the heart of the believer, and there are no prophecies left unfulfilled. There's only one problem with that position. It does not harmonize with the rest of the Bible.

Take a good look at the picture below. This is a picture for the image the king saw in a dream in the day of Daniel. You can read the while story in Daniel 2.

The king was upset because he couldn't understand what this "nightmare" was all about. But thank God, Daniel was called in and God gave him the interpretation.

The image in Daniel, chapter 2, gave us a picture of every world kingdom from the time of Babylon until the Second Coming of Christ to set up His earthly Kingdom.

The stone, which represents Christ, did not come during the **Babylonian Empire.**

Jesus did not come and set up His Kingdom in the days of the **Persian Empire.**

Jesus did not come and set up His Kingdom in the days of the **Greek Empire.**

Jesus did not come and set up His Kingdom in the days of

the **Roman Empire** (legs of iron).

"In those days, will the God of heaven set up a kingdom that shall never be destroyed." (Daniel 2:44)

There will be a ten nation federation in the latter days, and Christ will return in the days of those kings and will set up a kingdom that shall never be destroyed." **Read Daniel 2 again.**

Jesus will return in the days of the FEET. The feet are ten nations that will have come out of the Roman Empire (Europe).

The stone is Jesus. Jesus will return in the days of the FEET and set up His Kingdom.

THE FINAL REBELLION (Rev. 20:7-9)

"Now when the thousand years have expired, Satan will be released from his prison and will go out to deceive the nations which are in the four corners of the earth, Gog and Magog, to gather them together to battle, whose number is as the sand of the sea.

They went up on the breadth of the earth and surrounded the camp of the saints and the beloved city.

And fire came down from God out of heaven and devoured them."

THREE MAJOR WARS COMING

1. The battle of Gog and Magog (Ezekiel 38-39),

2. The Battle of Armageddon (Rev. 19),

3. The Final Rebellion (Rev. 20:7-9).

This battle in chapter 20 is the third and final battle of history. The following is a summary of this battle.

Satan will be loosed from his prison for a short period of time (season).

Satan will go back to his work of deceiving the nations. Satan will gather a following of rebels who had been born during the Millennium.

These rebels will have been born from parents who had been allowed to enter the Kingdom in their natural bodies.

These rebels are like children who have been born in Christian homes, attended Christian Schools, yet still reject the truth and rebel against God.

Don't Confuse this Gog and Magog

Some have confused Gog and Magog here with Gog and Magog in Ezekiel 38-39. There is a difference. This is important.

1. In Ezekiel, they come from the North. In Rev. 20, they come from all over the world.

2. In Ezekiel, God destroys all but 1/6 of the armies that come against Israel. In Rev. 20, God leaves no survivors.

3. In Ezekiel, it takes 7 months to bury the dead. In Rev. 20, there is nothing left to bury!

The Final Doom of Satan (Rev. 20:10)

"The devil, who deceived them, was cast into the lake of fire and brimstone where the beast and the false prophet are. And they will be tormented day and night forever and ever."

Everything in this verse is literal. The Devil is real; the lake of fire is real. The brimstone is real. The Beast is real. The False Prophet is real. And the torment is real, and the duration is real. Satan's followers will be there soon, but he is the first one there because hell was made for him.

THE GREAT WHITE THRONE JUDGMENT

(Rev. 20:11-14) *"Then I saw a great white throne and Him who sat on it, from whose face the earth and the heaven fled away. And there was found no place for them.*

And I saw the dead, small and great, standing before God, and books were opened. And another book was opened, which is the Book of Life. And the dead were judged according to their works, by the things which were written in the books.

The sea gave up the dead who were in it, and Death and Hades delivered up the dead who were in them. And they were judged, each one according to his works. Then Death and Hades were cast into the lake of fire. This is the second death."

1. Lost Sinners Only

This is for sinners only. Believers have already been judged. Our sins were judged at Calvary and our works were judged at the "Bema Seat of Christ" (2 Corinthians 5:10).

2. Bodies and Souls

The sinners' body and soul will be reunited. Their bodies will be raised from their graves and their souls will be called up out of hell[120] and they will stand before Christ.

---

[120]Literally "Hades." The realm of the dead.

3. The Judge

Jesus Christ will be their judge. (John 5:22) "For the Father judges no one, but has committed all judgment to the Son."

4. Two Books

Two books will be opened in the sinners' judgment. One is the book of works in which God has recorded every act, every word, every deed, and every thought from the cradle to the grave. The other book is the Book of Life in which God has recorded he names of all who are saved.

5. The Lake of Fire

This judgment concludes with sinners, the grave, and the present hell (hades) all cast into the Lake of Fire where they will all spend eternity in eternal torment.

THIS IS THE END OF ALL HUMAN HISTORY. AT THIS POINT, WE ENTER ETERNITY!

CHAPTER 21

THE NEW HEAVENS AND NEW EARTH

We've now come to the end of The Revelation and the end of all human history. From this point on we are dealing with eternity and our information on this is limited.

Actually there is much more information on the eternal state of sinners than there is on the eternal state of those who are saved? However, we have been given enough information about our eternal state to help us get fully prepared.

Let's read about that future heaven and earth God has promised for the future.

(Revelation 21:1) *1"Now I saw a new heaven and a new earth, for the first heaven and the first earth had passed away. Also there was no more sea."*

Coming Meltdown (2 Peter 3:10-13)

How will the present heaven and earth pass away? Peter predicted that the present heaven and earth will one day pass away, in what may be described as a total "meltdown." *"But the day of the Lord will come as a thief in the night, in which the heavens will pass away with a great noise, and the elements will melt with fervent heat; both the earth and the works that are in it will be burned up.*

A Sobering Question

11 Therefore, since all these things will be dissolved, what manner of persons ought you to be in holy conduct and godliness,

12 looking for and hastening the coming of the day of God, because of which the heavens will be dissolved, being on fire, and the elements will melt with fervent heat?

A new world is coming

13 Nevertheless we, according to His promise, look for new heavens and a new earth in which righteousness dwells.

14 Therefore, beloved, looking forward to these things, be diligent to be found by Him in peace, without spot and blameless;"

No more sea

The Holy Spirit reveled to John that there will be no oceans on the new earth. This is interesting in view of the fact that at the present time, 3/4 of the earth's surface is covered with water, making it uninhabitable. In eternity, the entire (new) earth will be habitable.

When will this happen?

Some scholars believe chapters 21 and 22 describe the Millennium.

We believe these chapters describe the eternal state. For example:

- In the Millennium, Jesus will reign in the Old

Jerusalem. In eternity, Jesus will reign in the New Jerusalem.

- In the Millennium, there will be large bodies of water.

- In the eternal state there will be no oceans.

- In the Millennium, there will be a temple. In eternity there is no temple (Rev. 21:22).

- In the Millennium, men will live longer but those in mortal bodies will eventually die. In eternity there is no dying (Rev. 21:4).

- Peter states clearly that God will create new heavens and a new earth.

The New Jerusalem (Rev.21:2-4)

2 Then I, John, saw the holy city, New Jerusalem, coming down out of heaven from God, prepared as a bride adorned for her husband.

3 And I heard a loud voice from heaven saying, "Behold, the tabernacle of God is with men, and He will dwell with them, and they shall be His people. God Himself will be with them and be their God.

4 And God will wipe away every tear from their eyes; there shall be no more death, nor sorrow, nor crying. There shall be no more pain, for the former things have passed away.

The New Jerusalem is not created in this passage

It was in existence during the Millennium. At this point, the New Jerusalem will be seen coming down and will be

317

suspended above the earth like a satellite.

- During the Millennium, the saints, in their translated bodies will probably travel back and forth from there to the earth which will be inhabited by people who are still in their mortal bodies.

- We believe the New Jerusalem, which is suspended above the earth like a satellite, will be moved away briefly for the "meltdown" and then brought back near the new earth and remain there for eternity.

Abraham

This is the city Abraham looked for while he was living in a tent (Hebrews 11:9-16).

The Size

The Heavenly City will be larger than the moon. The city will be a cube within a sphere. We will live on the inside and the first floor alone will be large enough to hold 170 times the present world population.

Everything New

5 Then He who sat on the throne said, "Behold, I make all things new." And He said to me, "Write, for these words are true and faithful."

6 And He said to me, "It is done! I am the Alpha and the Omega, the Beginning and the End. I will give of the fountain of the water of life freely to him who thirsts.

7 He who overcomes shall inherit all things, and I will be his God and he shall be My son."

Who won't be there?

8 But the cowardly, unbelieving, abominable, murderers, sexually immoral, sorcerers, idolaters, and all liars shall have their part in the lake which burns with fire and brimstone, which is the second death."

- Cowards,

- Unbelievers,

- Abominable,

- Murderers,

- Sexually immoral,

- Sorcerers,

- Idolaters, and

- All liars shall have their part in the lake which burns with fire and brimstone, which is the second death." This is serious business.

Description of the New Jerusalem (Rev. 21:9-27)

9 Then one of the seven angels who had the seven bowls filled with the seven last plagues came to me and talked with me, saying, "Come, I will show you the bride, the Lamb's wife."

10 And he carried me away in the Spirit to a great and high mountain, and showed me the great city, the holy Jerusalem, descending out of heaven from God,

11 having the glory of God. Her light was like a most precious stone, like a jasper stone, clear as crystal.

12 Also she had a great and high wall with twelve gates, and twelve angels at the gates, and names written on them, which are the names of the twelve tribes of the children of Israel:

13 three gates on the east, three gates on the north, three gates on the south, and three gates on the west.

14 Now the wall of the city had twelve foundations, and on them were the names of the twelve apostles of the Lamb.

15 And he who talked with me had a gold reed to measure the city, its gates, and its wall.

16 The city is laid out as a square; its length is as great as its breadth. And he measured the city with the reed: twelve thousand furlongs. Its length, breadth, and height are equal.

17 Then he measured its wall: one hundred and forty-four cubits, according to the measure of a man, that is, of an angel.

18 The construction of its wall was of jasper; and the city was pure gold, like clear glass.

19 The foundations of the wall of the city were adorned with all kinds of precious stones: the first foundation was jasper, the second sapphire, the third chalcedony, the fourth emerald,

20 the fifth sardonyx, the sixth sardius, the seventh chrysolite, the eighth beryl, the ninth topaz, the tenth chrysoprase, the eleventh jacinth, and the twelfth amethyst.

21 The twelve gates were twelve pearls: each individual gate was of one pearl. And the street of the city was pure gold, like transparent glass.

No temple there (Rev. 21:21-27)

21 And the twelve gates were twelve pearls: every several gate was of one pearl: and the street of the city was pure gold, as it were transparent glass.

22 And I saw no temple therein: for the Lord God Almighty and the Lamb are the temple of it.

23 And the city had no need of the sun, neither of the moon, to shine in it: for the glory of God did lighten it, and the Lamb is the light thereof.

24 And the nations of them which are saved shall walk in the light of it: and the kings of the earth do bring their glory and honor into it.

25 And the gates of it shall not be shut at all by day: for there shall be no night there.

26 And they shall bring the glory and honor of the nations into it.

27 And there shall in no wise enter into it anything that defileth, neither whatsoever worketh abomination, or maketh a lie: but they which are written in the Lamb's book of life."

CHAPTER 22

ETERNITY WITH OUR SAVIOR

A River of Life

1 And he showed me a pure river of water of life, clear as crystal, proceeding from the throne of God and of the Lamb.

2 In the middle of its street, and on either side of the river, was the tree of life, which bore twelve fruits, each tree yielding its fruit every month. The leaves of the tree were for the healing of the nations.

3 And there shall be no more curse, but the throne of God and of the Lamb shall be in it, and His servants shall serve Him.

4 They shall see His face, and His name shall be on their foreheads.

No Night and No Sun

5 There shall be no night there: They need no lamp nor light of the sun, for the Lord God gives them light. And they shall reign forever and ever.

God's Words are true

6 Then he said to me, "These words are faithful and true." And the Lord God of the holy prophets sent His angel to show His servants the things which must shortly take place.

7 "Behold, I am coming quickly! Blessed is he who keeps the words of the prophecy of this book."

Don't worship angels

8 Now I, John, saw and heard these things. And when I heard and saw, I fell down to worship before the feet of the angel who showed me these things.

9 Then he said to me, "See that you do not do that. For I am your fellow servant, and of your brethren the prophets, and of those who keep the words of this book. Worship God."

10 And he said to me, "Do not seal the words of the prophecy of this book, for the time is at hand.

11 He who is unjust, let him be unjust still; he who is filthy, let him be filthy still; he who is righteous, let him be righteous still; he who is holy, let him be holy still."

12 "And behold, I am coming quickly, and My reward is with Me, to give to every one according to his work.

13 I am the Alpha and the Omega, the Beginning and the End, the First and the Last."

14 Blessed are those who do His commandments, that they may have the right to the tree of life, and may enter through the gates into the city.

God's last warning

15 But outside are dogs and sorcerers and sexually immoral and murderers and idolaters, and whoever loves and practices a lie.

16 *"I, Jesus, have sent My angel to testify to you these things in the churches. I am the Root and the Offspring of David, the Bright and Morning Star."*

God's last invitation

17 *And the Spirit and the bride say, "Come!" And let him who hears say, "Come!" And let him who thirsts come. Whoever desires, let him take the water of life freely.*

Don't tamper with God's Word

18 *For I testify to everyone who hears the words of the prophecy of this book: If anyone adds to these things, God will add to him the plagues that are written in this book;*

19 *and if anyone takes away from the words of the book of this prophecy, God shall take away his part from the Book of Life, from the holy city, and from the things which are written in this book.*

LOOK UP! JESUS IS COMING AGAIN!

20 *He who testifies to these things says, "Surely I am coming quickly." Amen. Even so, come, Lord Jesus!*

21 *The grace of our Lord Jesus Christ be with you all. Amen.*

REDEMPTION DRAWETH NIGH

Years of time have come and gone
Since I first heard it told
How Jesus would come again some day
If back then it seemed so real
Then I just can't help but feel
How much closer His coming is today

Chorus:
Signs of the times are everywhere
There's a brand new feeling in the air
Keep your eyes upon the eastern sky
Lift up your head redemption draweth nigh

Wars and strife on every hand
And violence fills the land
Still some people doubt He'll ever come again
But the Word of God is true
He'll redeem His chosen few
Don't lose hope soon Christ Jesus will descend

Author Unknown

WHAT WE BELIEVE

1. I believe Jesus is coming back. His return is literal and future.

2. There are no "signs" that must be fulfilled before He comes.

3. His coming is imminent. This means He could come soon, or He could come 20 years from now.

4. I believe He is coming FOR His people. This is called the "Rapture."

5. Those who are saved will be taken. Those who are lost will be left behind to endure the 7 year tribulation.

6. During that 7 year Tribulation period, those who are saved will stand before the Judgment Seat of Christ (2 Cor. 5:10)

7. Those who are left behind will either believe the lie of Anti-Christ, or be saved, refuse his mark, and die as martyrs.

SOME BELIEVE WE ARE CONFUSED

Some time ago a Preterist friend of mine posted the following picture on Facebook. He knows I am not a Preterist and suggested that those who believe like I do are confused. I decided not to respond and he later removed the picture.

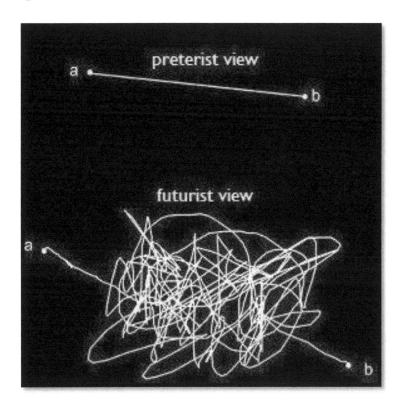

Here are some Questions

If you really believe Christ returned in 70 AD, that Satan is bound, and we are now in the Kingdom. If that is true, then what of the dozens of prohecies that have not been fulfilled? Did God simply cancel those prophecies or what? Here are some questions for serious thought.

1. When was the Gospel preached to all the nations?

2. When was the Mark of the Beast implemented?

3. How could Nero be the anti-Christ? He never sat in the temple and demanded worship? He never required a mark on people's hand or forehead. He didn't have a deadly wound that was healed. Nero was a wimpy emperor who committed suicide.

4. What date was it when the Euphrates River dried up?

5. When did China's 200-million-man army march across the Euphrates?

6. When did 100-pound hailstones fall from the sky?

7. They say that although the "resurrection" happened in 70 AD, the bodies of Christians were left in the grave. The questions are endless.

8. Why did we have the rebirth of Israel? If Jerusalem was forever removed from being the burdensome stone, why has it now returned to that status?

9. When did all the Jews shout, "Blessed is he who comes in the name of the Lord," as Jesus said they would?

10. When did the elements (earth, sun, moon, stars, etc.) melt with fervent heat?

11. Preterists take the dangerous step of spiritualizing all passages of Scripture that relate to the nation of Israel, and claim that these refer to the church, the "New Israel."

They teach that the "old earth," which Scripture says will pass away, is the Old Covenant. The new heaven and new earth, they say, is the New Covenant, and the "elements," which Scripture says will burn with fervent heat when this happens, are the "elements of the law."

2 Peter 3:9-15

Here is what the Bible says will happen, and in my opinion, has not happened yet. The literal elements will melt with literal fervent heat: 2 Peter 3:9-15 King James Version (KJV)

9 The Lord is not slack concerning his promise, as some men count slackness; but is longsuffering to us-ward, not willing that any should perish, but that all should come to repentance.

10 But the day of the Lord will come as a thief in the night; in which the heavens shall pass away with a great noise, and the elements shall melt with fervent heat, the earth also and the works that are therein shall be burned up.

11 Seeing then that all these things shall be dissolved, what manner of persons ought ye to be in all holy conversation and godliness,

12 looking for and hasting unto the coming of the day of God, wherein the heavens being on fire shall be dissolved, and the elements shall melt with fervent heat?

13 Nevertheless we, according to his promise, look for new heavens and a new earth, wherein dwelleth righteousness.

14 Wherefore, beloved, seeing that ye look for such things, be diligent that ye may be found of him in peace, without spot, and blameless.

I will let you be the judge of who is confused and who is not. If you believe Christ returned in 70 AD, that Satan is bound, and we are now in the Kingdom. If that is true, then what of the dozens of prophecies that have not been fulfilled?

PS While trying to decide whether Daniel and the Revelation have any message for the future, or any prophecies that have not yet been fulfilled, I suggest you read the twelfth chapter of Daniel. The Holy Spirit gave Daniel the message and then told Daniel to "seal up his book" until the latter days. This means that no one would be able to understand his message until the last days.

(Daniel 12:4,8,9)

4 But thou, O Daniel, **shut up the words, and <u>seal the book, even to the time of the end</u>:** many shall run to and fro, and knowledge shall be increased. 8 And I heard, but I understood not: then said I, O my Lord, what shall be the end of these things? **9 And he said, go thy way, Daniel: for the words are <u>closed up and sealed</u> till the time of the end**.

We Report! You Decide!!

ABOUT THE AUTHOR

Gene is part of a ten generation legacy of pioneer Christian leaders from Kentucky, Texas, and Florida. The following quote is from an article which appeared in the Florida Baptist Witness January 28, 2013. The article was titled, "Circling the Wagons" by Joni B. Hannigan, Managing Editor.

GAINESVILLE (FBW) — *The woods weren't safe around Ten Mile Creek settlements and so when families gathered for worship, John Keith, an elder in the Baptist church, made sure they met inside the rough-hewn logs of his private fort. Since 1773 when John Keith hosted the first meeting of Virginia's Ten Mile Baptist Church, the Keith men for at least ten generations have led their congregations as Baptist preachers, elders or deacons — to be pioneers in sharing the Gospel. By wagon, on horseback, on foot, and by car, they've traveled carrying the Good News of Christ from the thick forests of Virginia, across the green mountains of Kentucky, to the High Plains of Texas before finally turning back southeast to settle in sun-drenched Central Florida where three generations now pastor two churches just 20 miles apart. Coming together on Christmas day, Gene, Bill and Billy Keith — father, son and grandson — took part in an 80/60/40 service marking their 2012 birthdays and celebrating a common heritage in ministry.*

Gene was born William Eugene Keith in Tarpon Springs, Florida on Christmas Day, 1932. He attended School in Tarpon Springs, played football for the Spongers, first trumpet in the band, and graduated in 1950. He attended Stetson University, the University of Florida, and received his BA from Luther Rice.

Gene and his wife, the former Tuelah Evelyn Riviere, celebrated their sixty first wedding anniversary in 2013. They have six children thirty Grandchildren, and thirty-three Great grandchildren (with three more the way). Gene loves writing, fishing, hunting, and spending time with his family.

Gene has a wide range of experience, having served as Pastor, School Principal, Country Music DJ, radio talk show host, and a Consultant for Christian Education.

Gene Keith is presently Pastor Emeritus of the Countryside Baptist Church of Gainesville, having served there since 1959, with the exception of two years during which he served as pastor of First Baptist Church of Cape Canaveral when America sent the first men to the moon. He retired in 2010 and his son, Bill is now the pastor of Countryside.

Gene turned 81 on Christmas day 2013 and spends most of his time writing and speaking. For information on Gene's books please contact us at: gk122532@gmail.com

SELECTED BIBLIOGRAPHY

John Walvoord, The Revelation of Jesus Christ, (Chicago: Moody Press,1966)

Ray Summers, Worthy is the Lamb (Nashville: Broadman Press, 1951)

Loraine Boettner, New Testament Survey (Grand Rapids: The Presbyterian and Reformed Publishing Company,)

Vernon McGee, Thru the Bible Commentary, Vol. V (Nashville: Thomas Nelson Publishers, 1983)

Charles Ryrie, Ryrie Study Bible (Chicago: Moody Press, 1986)

Walid Shoebat http://shoebat.com/2013/05/31/mystery-babylon-is-mecca-not-vatican/

This study was prepared and taught by Pastor Gene Keith in 2007 in the Countryside Baptist Church of Gainesville, Florida and first published in December 2013.

11546907R00191

Made in the USA
San Bernardino, CA
21 May 2014